Roman Slave Law

Alan Watson

Roman Slave Law

The Johns Hopkins University Press
Baltimore and London

© 1987 The Johns Hopkins University Press
All rights reserved
Printed in the United States of America

The Johns Hopkins University Press
701 West 40th Street
Baltimore, Maryland 21211
The Johns Hopkins Press Ltd., London

The paper used in this publication meets the minimum requirements
of American National Standard for Information Sciences—Permanence
of Paper for Printed Library Materials, ANSI Z39.48-1984.

Library of Congress Cataloging-in-Publication Data
Watson, Alan.
  Roman slave law.

  Bibliography: p.
  Includes index.
  1. Slavery (Roman law) I. Title.
KJA2198.W38 1987   346.3701'3   86-21351
                     343.70613
ISBN 0-8018-3439-2 (alk. paper)

For Camilla

Contents

Foreword

Although Alan Watson reluctantly chose not to focus upon the explicit comparisons between the Roman law of slavery and American slave law, for the student or scholar of American slavery his study of Roman slave law is implicitly comparative at every point, and importantly so. Each issue explored in this work reveals a significant aspect of the law of slavery wherever it has been found, and the Roman system of "colorblind oppression" offers an invaluable reference point—a racially neutral slavery system—against which the devastating oppression born of the color-consciousness of America's fundamentally racist breed of slavery may be evaluated and better understood. This work places the Roman law of slavery well within the reach of all who endeavor to analyze and understand slavery as a human phenomenon as well as those who seek to study America's historically peculiar form of slavery and its continuing impact and significance for contemporary American race relations law.

Professor Watson's self-proclaimed mission is to explore how the Romans used the law to maximize the benefits of slavery for the slaveholder. This was done, in his words, by "maximizing the profit (economic, social, and political) and minimizing the risk (economic and physical)." Watson asserts that the way in which any society pursues this task "will depend in large measure on the criteria adopted to determine who is a slave and who is free." This leads to the suggestion that variations in the substantive provisions of the law of slavery in ancient Rome and in the United States were produced not only by the different social, political, and economic contexts of the two slave systems, but perhaps more so by the fact that the central criterion for determining whether a person would be a slave in America was skin color, while in Rome enslavement was not based upon race or background, but was "a misfortune that could happen to anyone."

A reading of this significant study reveals that a central contrast between the nonracially (and nonethnically) based Roman slavery and the racially based slavery of the American colonies and, later, the United States was precisely the issue addressed by Chief Justice Roger Brooke Taney in the infamous Dred Scott case—whether, under the Constitution of that era, a free black could ever be a citizen of the United States and entitled to the range of rights and privileges annexed to that status. Most Roman slaves were welcomed to the status of citizen upon being freed and, indeed, had that possibility held out to them during their enslavement as an inducement to work to the greatest benefit of their owners. In stark contrast, under the Dred Scott decision, freed blacks could not be United States citizens and, further, "had no rights which the white man was bound to respect."[1]

Perhaps at the core of this difference—and at the core of the contrast between the racist and colorblind systems—lies the perception so central to the American peculiar institution, that blacks (and, hence, slaves) were inferior. Professor Watson notes that the Roman status of slave carried with it no necessary implication that the slave was an inferior being. While a Roman slave "might be extremely well educated . . . or be profoundly ignorant, outstandingly clever, or rather stupid," the assumed inferiority of the black slave was a central tenet of the American system. The American law of slavery not only embodied and reinforced the perception, but also denied blacks the opportunity to rebut the presumption of inferiority by precluding them from managing their own affairs or developing significant professional and intellectual skills. Many states went so far as to make it a crime to teach a slave to read or write.[2] Similarly, while a Roman slave "might be expected to work as a doctor; run a business; act as general business agent for his master; [or] be an artist [or] gladiator," the laws of American slavery severely restricted slaves from engaging in business, the professions, or commercial transactions. For example, South Carolina's slave code of 1751 prohibited the employment of slaves in an apothecary for fear they would learn about poisons. Slaves were also prohibited from being doctors out of a fear that they would use the opportunity to convey insurrectionary plots or other "dangerous information." The code also prohibited slaves from dealing in rice or corn in an attempt to reduce the incentive for slaves to steal.[3]

Similarly, in Virginia, only free white citizens were allowed to pilot vessels in the Rappahannock River,[4] and the following statute imposed a penalty on those who bought tobacco from a black person:

> Every stemmer or manufacturer who shall buy or receive any tobacco from any negro, mulatto or Indian, (bond or free) shall forfeit and pay five times the value of the tobacco so bought or received, and shall moreover be liable to be prosecuted as a receiver of stolen goods, provided the same shall be stolen tobacco.[5]

Another important contrast between the two systems emerges. Watson points out that, according to Justinian's *Institutes*, "the principal distinction in the law of persons is that all men are either free or slaves—there is no third, intermediate, category." The racially-based American law of slavery produced just such a third, intermediate category—that of the free black, who seemed to be suspended in a legal limbo somewhere between slavery and true freedom. This stands in stark contrast to the status of ex-slaves of Rome, who could, under certain circumstances, receive the full panoply of citizenship rights. Free blacks in the pre–Civil War United States were not given the full range of rights enjoyed by white citizens, and the question of their citizenship status and privileges was often debated in the courts. In 1837, the Supreme Court of the Quaker-dominated northern state of Pennsylvania considered whether blacks were entitled to vote under the constitution and laws of the commonwealth. The court declared:

It is to be remembered that citizenship as well as freedom, is a constitutional qualification; and how it could be conferred so as to overbear the laws imposing countless disabilities on him in other states, is a problem of difficult solution. . . . Every man must lament the necessity of these disabilities; but slavery is to be dealt with by those whose existence depends on the skill with which it is treated. Considerations of mere humanity, however, belong to a class with which, as judges, we have nothing to do; and interpreting the constitution in the spirit of our institutions, we are bound to pronounce that men of colour are destitute of title to the elective franchise. Their blood, however, may become so diluted in successive descents as to lose its distinctive character; and, then, both policy and justice require that previous disabilities should cease.[6]

The intermediate status of "free" blacks was discussed at length by Chief Justice Taney in the Dred Scott case. He devoted a substantial portion of his opinion to a review of the myriad of "disabilities" imposed by law upon blacks in the several states in order to demonstrate their lack of a claim to citizenship status. Taney fortified his argument by citing statutes from northern states "where slavery had worn out or measures [had been] taken for its speedy abolition." He first noted Massachussetts laws prohibiting interracial marriage. Turning to Connecticut, he cited a statute that treated free negroes and servants similarly by providing that "any negro, Indian or mulatto servant, who was found wandering out of the town or place to which he belonged, without a written pass" was liable to be seized by anyone and taken before the authorities. The same enactment also provided that *free* negroes traveling without passes were responsible for paying all related charges if they were "stopped, seized or taken up." Finally, Taney referred us to Chief Justice Daggett's decision in *Crandall* v. *The State*[7] that persons of the African race "were not citizens of a State, within the meaning of the word citizen in the Constitution of the United States, and were not therefore entitled to the privileges and immunities of citizens in other States." Additionally, New Hampshire limited membership in the militia to free white citizens. Having marshalled the evidence in this way, Taney is led to his conclusion that "the legislation of the states therefore shows, in a manner not to be mistaken, the inferior and subject condition of that race."[8]

The reader familiar with American law will recognize numerous other familiar issues and characteristics of American slavery—among them the sexism contained in laws enacted in both systems that viewed a free woman's union with a slave man less favorably than a free man's union with a slave woman. Both systems provided distinctly harsher punishment to the free woman who dared to enter such a relationship. Though American slave law on the subject embodied blatantly racist values along with its sexism, intriguingly enough, this sexism was also present in Roman slave law, though, as Professor Watson points out, Roman law was "colorblind" and never prohibited interracial sexual relationships or marriage. Both were restricted by the American colonies and states. For example, Virginia prohibited interracial marriage as early as 1691[9] and, as Chief Justice Taney pointed out in the Dred Scott case, Massachusetts did the same in its statutes of 1705 and 1786, as well as in its revised code of 1836.[10]

An important aspect of the analysis of any slave system is a consideration of the conflicts between the legal recognition of the slave as both person and property. This is a point of commonality between the law of slavery in Rome and the United States. In chapter 4, Professor Watson considers the legal treatment of the slave as a "thing" similar to other "things" that were subject to ownership. Although aspects of the slave's humanity emerged in other areas of law that recognized the slave's possession of human will (notably the treatment of the slave's culpability under the criminal law), as a thing the slave was treated as another species of property that had a monetary value and could be bought and sold under the same property laws as cattle and other animals.

Among the concerns expressed in the law of both slavery systems are the conditions of sale and exchange of slave property. One notable area is that of warranties against defects, and the question of which of the conditions to which a human species of property is subject would be accorded legal recognition as giving rise to a legally cognizable claim by the buyer against the seller. The commercial law of slavery is an area of American slave law that has not been adequately explored, and Professor Watson's survey of the treatment of these issues in the Roman law can serve as a valuable starting point in a review of the topics that profitably could be considered. These include the question of the civil liability of one who causes injury to the slave property of another through willful or negligent behavior; theft of slaves; and another concern of American slavery so central that it was embodied in one of the great compromises of the United States Constitution when it was drafted in 1787—the treatment of runaway or fugitive slaves. In each of these areas, the slave's capacities and identity as a human form of property caused lawmakers to stretch and bend "normal" rules of property law to meet the unique situations posed.

The slave's humanity posed an additional dilemma for the law of slavery in both societies by raising the question of who would be held legally responsible for a slave's actions or misdeeds—the slave himself or herself, or the slave owner. These questions are considered by Professor Watson in chapter 5, "The Slave as Man: Noncommercial Relations." Additional issues are the regulation of marriage and personal relationships (slaves could not legally marry in ancient Rome or in the United States), and the status of slaves as witnesses, accusers, and the accused in criminal proceedings.

A particularly heinous aspect of American slavery was the lack of protection of the slave from physical punishment or abuse by the master or a stranger. Several slave jurisdictions wrestled with the apparently confusing question whether it was a crime to kill a slave, and what the standards of assault against a slave would be.[11] Here we enter into the domain of what Professor Watson describes as "moral squeamishness": "What limits does a society that accepts the social institution of slavery place on enslavement, on the treatment of slaves, and on the rewarding of slaves because of humanitarian considerations?" Neither Roman nor American slave society score very high on the scale of humanitarian considerations in the protection of the slave from abuse that would have been considered assault or murder if committed against a nonslave. This section is a most convincing demonstration of the truth of Professor Watson's statement that "nonracist slavery is very different but may be no less horrifying in many respects than racist slavery. The rewards offered to 'good' slaves may be greater, but punishment of slaves by masters may be no more restrained."

Jurists and legal scholars in both Rome and the new American nation acknowledged that slavery was contrary to natural law. But just how contrary to natural law protections of personal safety and of personal liberty each system was can be horrifying to confront. Though deeply disturbing, both for what it reveals about Roman slavery as well as what it implicitly reveals about America's peculiar institution, Alan Watson's study is a thorough, extensively-documented, insightful, and refreshingly readable account which more than lives up to its own promise to make "a contribution to understanding slave law in the United States, the effect of racism, and the nature of slavery."[8]

Notes

I am deeply indebted to Laura B. Farmelo, Esq. for her contribution to this Foreword, which, in many ways, we have coauthored.

1. *Dred Scott* v. *Sanford,* 60 U.S. 393, 407 (1857).
2. For example, the following provision of the Virginia Code of 1848 made it a crime not only for slaves, but for any blacks, to assemble for the purpose of learning to read or write:

   Every assemblage of negroes for the purpose of instruction in reading or writing shall be an unlawful assembly. Any justice may issue his warrant to any officer or other person requiring him to enter any place where such an assembly may be and seize any Negro therein; and any other justice may order such a Negro to be punished with stripes.

   If a white person assemble with negroes for the purpose of instructing them to read or write, he shall be confined to jail not exceeding six months and fined not exceeding one hundred dollars.(*Va. Code* [1848], pp. 747–48)

3. *Statutes at Large of South Carolina,* vol. 7, pp. 397, 433. Also, see generally A. Leon Higginbotham, Jr., *In the Matter of Color: Race and the American Legal Process: The Colonial Period* (New York: Oxford University Press, 1978) for further restrictions on slave activities and occupations.
4. *Laws of Virginia,* Chapter 61 (1826).
5. Ibid., Chapter 64 (1801).
6. *Hobbs* v. *Fogg,* 6 Watts 553, 560 (1837).
7. 10 Conn. Rep. 340 (1884).
8. 60 U.S. 353, 415, and 416.

9. The preamble to the 1691 act states that the purpose of the statute was to prevent "that abominable mixture and spurious issue . . . by Negroes, mulattoes and Indians intermarrying with English or other white women." It provided that "whatsoever English or other white man or woman, bond or free, shall intermarry with a Negro, mulatto, or Indian man or woman, bond or free, he shall within three months be banished from this dominion forever," [Act XVI, William W. Hening, *Statutes at Large of Virginia,* Vol. 3, pp. 86–88]. See Higginbotham, *In the Matter of Color,* pp. 44–45.

10. Chief Justice Taney noted that:

The [Massachusetts] law of 1786, like the law of 1705, forbids the marriage of any white person with any negro, Indian, or mulatto, and inflicts a penalty of fifty pounds upon any one who shall join them in marriage; and declares all such marriages absolutely null and void, and degrades thus the unhappy issue of the marriage by fixing upon it the stain of bastardy. And this mark of degradation was renewed and again impressed upon the race, in the careful and deliberate preparation of their revised code published in 1836. This code forbids any person from joining in marriage any white person with any Indian, negro, or mulatto, and subjects the party who shall offend in this respect, to imprisonment, not exceeding six months, in the common jail, or to hard labor, and to a fine of not less than fifty nor more than two hundred dollars; and, like the law of 1786, it declares the marriage to be absolutely null and void. It will be seen that the punishment is increased by the code upon the person who shall marry them, by adding imprisonment to a pecuniary penalty. [60 U.S. 393, 413]

11. For example, the North Carolina Supreme Court grappled with these questions in a series of cases, including *State v. Boon,* 1 N.C. 246 (1801); *State v. Tackett,* 8 N.C. 210 (1820); *State v. Reed,* 9 N.C. 454 (1823); *State v. Hale,* 9 N.C. 582 (1823); *State v. Mann,* 13 N.C. 263 (1829); *State v. Will,* 18 N.C. 121 (1834); *State v. Hoover,* 20 N.C. 365 (1839); *State v. Jowers,* 33 N.C. 555 (1850); and *State v. Davis,* 52 N.C. 52 (1859).

A. LEON HIGGINBOTHAM, JR.

Preface

This book is not like others I have written on Roman law, which contain detailed analyses of all the source material on particular topics. Nor have I written for Roman law specialists.

The genesis of the book goes back to my first visit to the United States, to Louisiana in 1967, when I was struck by the very different configuration of the law of slavery in the American South and at Rome. I concluded that the principal reason for the difference lay in the inherently racist nature of Southern slavery, and I started writing this book in my own field to understand the Southern institution better. Hence the book is offered as a contribution to understanding slave law in the United States, the effect of racism, and the nature of slavery. This book is thus the converse of a volume on "*Hamlet* without the Prince of Denmark": it is about the Dred Scott case without his name being mentioned. Of course, I was also writing for those interested in Roman law or Roman society or law in general; in particular I wanted to stress Roman attitudes to law and to lawmaking and the special place of slavery law in a slave-owning society.

With these aims the main problem in writing the book was to get the balance right, and completed drafts in one form or another have surrounded me for years. They formed part of a course I have given from time to time entitled "The Law of Slavery: Ancient and Modern." In the end I decided to let the Roman texts speak for themselves and, to remain true to the Roman law, I give equal attention to rules that have little to say for Southern slavery. For the same reason, but with considerable doubts and hesitation, I have not brought forward explicit contrasts with U.S. law or with law in Spanish or French colonies. But here I should like to make two observations. First, nonracist slavery is very different but may be no less horrifying in many respects than racist slavery. The rewards offered to "good" slaves may be greater, but punishment of slaves by masters may be no more restrained. Second, the social institution of slavery in the Spanish and French possessions was no less racist than slavery in the United States, but the law in some regards looks much less so. The reason, I believe, is that French legal rules, such as those to be found in the *Codes Noirs,* were not generally written by the men on the ground but by men in Paris, at a great distance from the living phenomenon of slavery. The Spanish legal rules, in their turn, owe much to conditions in Spain, where slavery never disappeared from the law books.

The famous Harvard law professor Luther S. Cushing, discussing in 1854 the importance of Roman law after the fall of the Roman Empire, wrote:

> Its diffusion, from the middle ages to the present day, has taken place upon the simple principle, equally operative at this moment, that wherever, and whenever, and as to whatever, there was any want of its principles, for the regulation of human affairs, its authority has been at once recognized, admitted, and applied. An example of the Roman law occurs with reference to the institution of domestic slavery in this country. Wherever that relation has been introduced, it has been followed and regulated, in the absence of other legislation, by the principles of the Roman law.[1]

These are strong words on the impact of Roman law and may seem implausible to a modern reader. But Cushing was writing when slavery was well established in the South, and he was an expert on the law both of Rome and the United States. Moreover, Roman law was then well known in this country, especially in the South,[2] and references to Roman law do appear in judicial dicta in Southern slave cases. In large measure where, to us, Roman law and Southern slave law wear a very different guise, this is because the Roman rules were totally inappropriate for the very different social institution of slavery in the South. Or, perhaps, given the enormous influence of Roman law on subsequent Western law, it is not going too far to suggest that Southern slave law, when it did not adopt Roman rules, preferred others because of the power of racism.

To make the unfamiliar more accessible, a glossary and a chronology are appended to the end of this book.

Abbreviations

Buckland, *Slavery*	W. W. Buckland, *The Roman Law of Slavery* (Cambridge: Cambridge University Press, 1908).
C.	Justinian's *Codex* (Code)
Coll.	*Collatio Legum Mosaicarum et Romanarum* (Comparison of the laws of Moses and the Romans)
C.Th.	*Codex Theodosianus* (Theodosian code)
D.	Justinian's *Digestum* (Digest)
Epit. Ulp.	*Epitome Ulpiani* (Epitome of Ulpian)
Fabre, *Libertus*	*Recherches sur les rapports patron—affranchi à la fin de la République romaine* (Rome: Ecole Française de Rome, 1981)
fr. Dos.	*Fragmentum Dositheani* (Fragment attributed to Dositheanus)
Fr. Vat.	*Fragmenta Vaticana* (Vatican fragments)
G.	Gaius's *Institutes*
Gai Epit.	*Gai Epitome* (Epitome of Gaius)
J.	Justinian's *Institutes*
Kaser, *RPR*, 1, 2	M. Kaser, *Das römische Privatrecht*, 2 vols., 2d ed. (Munich: Beck, 1971, 1975)

Lenel, *Edictum*   O. Lenel, *Das Edictum Perpetuum,* 3d ed. (Leipzig: Tauschnitz, 1927)

P.S.   *Pauli Sententiae* (The Opinions of Paul)

T.v.R.   *Tijdschrift voor Rechtsgeschiedenis*

Watson, *Persons*   A. Watson, *The Law of Persons in the Later Roman Republic* (Oxford: Clarendon Press, 1967)

Watson, *XII Tables*   A. Watson, *Rome of the XII Tables: Persons and Property* (Princeton: Princeton University Press, 1975)

Roman Slave Law

Introduction

Slavery is an institution that operates on economic, moral, social, and political levels. The function of the law of slavery is to provide orderly and organized means of control of the resulting tensions. The central problem of slavery may be easily stated, and the issues that the law has to deal with succinctly set out. Slavery is the most extreme form imaginable of exploitation of one human being by another, but the exploitation need not always proceed in one direction alone. As a class and as individuals slaves are always exploited, but the individual slave is frequently in a good position to provide the master with a poor return on his investment, to cheat him, rob him, damage his property, or make him liable to others for property damage, to make disastrous contracts for him, to give damaging reports of him, to exploit him sexually, and even to assault or kill him. Moreover, the slave, exploited himself, has the clearest reason to exploit the master. The main question, then, is how to maximize the benefits of slavery for the owner.

What incentives, controls, or penalties are to be given by law to ensure that the slave does the best he can for the owner; best in the sense both of maximizing the profit (economic, social, and political) and of minimizing the risk (economic and physical)?[1] At the one extreme, the greatest inducement to the slave to benefit the

1

owner is the prospect of freedom and even citizenship, but how far can or should the state or society allow the master the right to introduce a new person into its midst? What other positive induce- ments for the slave to do his best for his master can be offered by law? At the other extreme, violence and punishment may seem to give the master greater satisfaction. But an unfettered freedom for masters to act cruelly to their slaves is bad for the members of the free society, not just morally but also economically, since resent- ment among the slaves may lead to repercussions. Long before Roman times Plato had declared that masters should treat their slaves with consideration, for the slaves' sake of course, but even more for the sake of the masters.[2] Yet for the free society at large as well as for the individual master it is useful that slaves generally obey orders. To what extent should the master's right to punish be fettered? The emphasis in the present book will be on how the Romans attempted to answer the questions of incentives and deterrents through rules of law. The answers for any society will depend in large measure on the criteria adopted to determine who is a slave and who is free. A subordinate question concerns moral squeamishness. What limits does a society that accepts the social institution of slavery place on enslavement, on the treatment of slaves, and on the rewarding of slaves because of humanitarian considerations?

The problem of slavery arises at Rome in its own particular way. For the whole period during which Rome is historically visible slaves were common. For the two centuries from around 200 B.C. when law most developed, the Roman economy was very largely based on conquest and slavery. For instance, Roman victories brought 150,000 Epirotes onto the Roman slave market in the year 167 B.C. alone. It is notoriously difficult to estimate numbers, but Keith Hopkins judges:

> According to the best modern estimates, there were about two (or even three) million slaves in Italy by the end of the first century B.C. That is about thirty five to forty per cent of the total estimated population of Italy. Given our evidence, these figures are only guesses; they may well be too large; when slavery was at its height in the southern states of the USA, the proportion of slaves was only one third. However that may be,

no one can reasonably doubt that huge numbers of slaves were imported into Italy during the last two centuries B.C. Roman Italy belonged to that very small group of five societies in which slaves constituted a large proportion of the labour force.[3]

Slaves could be of any race or background: other Italian peoples, Greeks, Syrians, Jews, Gauls, Britons, and so on, though there were relatively few black Africans. A slave might be extremely well educated from the Roman standpoint or be profoundly ignorant, outstandingly clever, or rather stupid. He might be expected to work as a doctor; run a business; act as general business agent for his master; be an artist, gladiator, or craftsman; be a house servant; or labor in the fields as one of a chain gang.[4] It is a characteristic of law that the same legal rules have to cope with a wide range of vastly different situations. In this case, law, being general, has to provide for slaves of all these categories and more. Slavery was a misfortune that could happen to anyone. However lowly the economic and social position of a slave might be, the slave was not necessarily and in all ways regarded as inferior as a human being simply because he was a slave. In keeping with this approach, the legal rules on slavery bear no sign of prejudice against racial or national groups (which is not to say that Rome was free from racism).[5] Just as significant for Roman attitudes is the fact that, by Roman law, a Roman captured by the enemy became a foreign slave and even lost his Roman citizenship. He might escape, of course, and return, whereupon some of his rights would revive to a greater or lesser extent. This whole topic of *postliminium,* as it is called, is so revealing—and at the same time contains so much subtle law—that some treatment of it will be given in this book.

The moral and economic nature of slavery is fundamentally affected by whether or not slavery is racist in character. If it is not, then the existence of slavery is not a statement of a world view of ethnic hierarchy. To be a slave is a misfortune for the individual, assuredly a grave one, but it is not inevitable, natural, or necessarily permanent. Except financially or socially, the slave need not be thought inferior to his master—indeed, there is no necessary obstacle to the notion that the slave may often be superior, morally, intellectually, and even in education. It is appropriate to entrust

3

tasks requiring great intellectual attainments and perhaps even moral delicacy to slaves. Obstacles to manumission may reasonably be fewer, and there is less of an incentive for denying citizenship to freed slaves.

Though Roman law has always been regarded as one of the great achievements of the human mind, the Roman jurists themselves almost always concentrated on very particular issues. Those responsible for the development of the law were not very interested in establishing a legal science or in developing general legal principles or in propounding high moral theory. Roman law progressed in the main through juristic consideration of innumerable individual situations, hypothetical as well as actual, with a continuing search for improved solutions. Roman slave law is part of Roman law. But the existence of slavery in a society raises particularly sensitive economic, humanitarian, and moral issues. The extent to which those concerned with the law treat legal rules of slavery as the same as, or different from, other kinds of legal rules reveals much about the human spirit, the attitudes of lawyers, and the notion of legality.

The rules of law that develop in any society are dependent on the means available for legal change. Hence a short account of the Roman legal sources is appropriate here.

At any period of Roman history law could be made by statute, though in fact at most times statutory law was rather uncommon. The earliest substantial body of law is in the archaic, earliest known Roman codification called the Twelve Tables of around 450 B.C. Legislation was passed by a Roman assembly, usually the *concilium plebis* (the assembly of the people) in the later Republic, and the *comitia centuriata* (the people in military array) under Augustus.

Of great importance were the Edicts of the magistrates, the elected public officials. All the higher magistrates had the power to make Edicts within their spheres of competence, setting out how they regarded their duties. The most important for us are those of the praetors, who controlled most of the important courts, and the curule aediles, who were in charge of the streets and markets. It became the practice for the praetors at the beginning of their year of office to put up a conspicuous notice in the forum saying how they would enforce the law. Technically they could not make law, but they could refuse to grant an established remedy, they could change the circumstances of an action, and they could even grant a totally new action. The praetors built on the work of their predecessors, and their Edicts were among the most important sources of law in the late Republic, though they lost their creativity in the early Empire and became fixed under Hadrian.

Decrees of the senate had no lawmaking force in the Republic, but in the early Empire they were often enforced by a clause inserted in the praetor's Edict, and under Hadrian they came to have direct lawmaking force.

Though there seems no legal foundation for it, the emperors could make law, whether by something akin to a statute, by decrees to provincial governors or other officials, or by *constitutiones* or rescripts (replies on points of law which had been raised by individuals).

The interpretation of the law was basically in the hands of jurists, individuals who felt confident enough in their own skill to give legal advice and write replies or even books. Such books were numerous from the first century B.C. to the third century A.D., and they took various forms: they might be collections of replies to legal problems or commentaries on a single topic or statute or on the whole of the civil law or praetor's Edict. None of those from the so-called classical period—before A.D. 235—has survived apart from Gaius's *Institutes,* an elementary text for beginners written in the late second century A.D. Two other juristic works are important for us: *Pauli Sententiae* (the Opinions of Paul), which is probably a postclassical collection of texts from this important jurist, and the *Collatio Legum Mosaicarum et Romanarum* (Comparison of the laws of Moses and the Romans), of uncertain origin but probably dating from around the beginning of the fifth century B.C.

Given the multiplicity of sources, it obviously was not always easy to know what the law was, and, after two unofficial collections, the *Codex Theodosianus* (Theodosian code), containing all the general imperial constitutions, was issued in A.D. 435.

When Justinian became Byzantine emperor in A.D. 527, he at once set himself to the task of restating the law. He had the imperial rescripts collected in the *Codex* (Code) which was issued in 529.

The first edition, which has not survived, was replaced by a second version in 534. Then he set up a commission to collect and abridge the writings of the classical jurists. The result, the *Digestum* (Digest), came into force as law in 533 together with the *Institutes,* a textbook for first-year students which was modeled on the *Institutes* of Gaius. The *Code,* the *Digest,* and the *Institutes,* with the subsequently published *Novellae* (New constitutions), promulgated after 534, came, in much later times, to be called the *Corpus Juris Civilis.*

The introduction into a society of slave labor on an enormous scale, as at Rome, has profound consequences which may or may not be obvious to contemporaries: the movement, for instance, away from the land by poor, free peasants, whether into the city or out of Italy altogether, and the increased wealth of the large landowner without the obvious exploitation of the free poor. These consequences will not be examined here.[6] The subject here is the law that arose directly from the social institution of slavery, the reasons for the choice of particular legal rules, and the attitudes that are revealed by the legal rules and contemporary discussion of them.

One

Enslavement

Justinian's *Institutes* tell us that the principal distinction in the law of persons is that all men are either free or slaves—there is no third, intermediate, category in Roman law (J.1.3.pr.). The emperor defines freedom as "the natural ability to do anything one wants unless it is prohibited by force or law" (J.1.3.1). To define freedom is notoriously difficult, and, as Buckland says, by this definition everyone would be free.[1] The failure to provide a better definition may stand as an illustration of the Roman lack of interest in definition. As the jurist Javolenus put it: "All definition in the civil law is dangerous: for it is seldom that a definition may not be turned upside down."[2] Justinian, then, following Florentinus, a jurist of the mid-second century,[3] defines slavery thus: "Slavery is an institution of the law of nations (*ius gentium*) by which, contrary to nature, a person is subjected to the dominion of another" (J.1.3.2). This is the only instance in Roman law in which a rule of the law of nations— defined as the law "which all nations obey" (J.1.2.1)—is said to be contrary to nature. No important practical consequences flow from the conflict—an indication of the lack of interest in, and unimportance of, an ideal law for the Romans. Significantly, perhaps, the definition's setting in life was an elementary textbook— Florentinus's *Institutiones*—and it also appears in Justinian's com-

7

pilation in that setting. Like definitions of *iustitia*[4] as the constant and perpetual desire to give each person his due, and of *iurispruden-tia*[5] as the knowledge of things divine and human, the science of the just and the unjust, and declarations of the precepts of the law such as "to live justly, not to injure another and to render each his own"[6]—so the declaration that slavery is an institution of the law of nations that is contrary to nature seems to be the sort of thing law professors say at the beginning of their courses to demonstrate awareness of the seriousness of their undertaking and forget about thereafter. Still, the definition betrays an uneasiness over the morality of slavery which may account for the placing of the next text both by Florentinus (D.1.5.4.2) and in Justinian's *Institutes* (J.1.3.3):

> Slaves (*servi*) are so called because commanders order captives to be sold and so spare (*servare*) rather than kill them: they are also called *mancipia* because they are taken physically (*manu capi*) from the enemy.

The correctness of the etymologies need not detain us, but the existence of the text just in this position suggests that slavery is being morally justified: slaves are persons who have received a benefit—their lives have been preserved when they would otherwise have been violently ended.

In fact, though capture in war had in the late Republic been a fruitful source of slaves, it had long ceased to be significant. Birth to a slave mother was, from at least the early Empire, the common source of slaves:

> D.1.5.5.1 (Marcian, first book of *Institutes*). Slaves are reduced to our ownership by civil law or by the law of nations: by the civil law if a person more than twenty years old allows himself to be sold to share in the price: those slaves are ours by the law of nations who are captured from the enemy or who are the offspring of our female slaves.

Civil law is that part of Roman law that is peculiar to the Romans or, at times, that part of Roman law in which foreigners do not participate. The point that Marcian seems to be making here is that the Roman law on enslavement contains rules that Roman law shares generally with other systems, as well as rules that are particular inventions of the Romans.

The rule, stated to be peculiarly Roman, that a free person who allowed himself to be sold as a slave in order to share in the price does become a slave is old, and derives from the fact that a free man cannot be distinguished from a slave by his appearance. The temptation to defraud was obviously not always resisted. A free man would act as if he were held as a slave and be sold by a friend who would disappear from the scene. A short time later the supposed slave would be "recognized" by another friend who would claim his liberty, and the friends, including the supposed slave, would share in the price. The Roman rule is an economical way of inhibiting frauds of this type. The free person became a slave only if he had actually received a share of the price[7] and only if the buyer had actually been deceived.[8] The law here originated in the praetor's Edict[9] and hence is most likely to be no more recent than the first century B.C.[10] The legal technique involved was that the praetor refused to allow the person who sold himself to make a claim of freedom (*proclamatio ad libertatem*). The penalty seems severe but it is directly related to the financial loss of the purchaser: he is allowed to keep as a slave the free person he bought who was fraudulently represented to be a slave. In the absence of an efficient police force to track down the other malefactors and recover the price, the solution is elegant if harsh. Under another clause of the Edict, a person less than twenty-five years old who entered an unfortunate transaction usually had the right to be restored to the position he would have been in but for the transaction. Nothing should be made of the fact that that clause usually did not apply where a free man had himself sold[11] or that in our case the age for supposed full responsibility was twenty, not twenty-five, because the more general edict usually did not apply[12] where the minor, as here, was fraudulent. More interesting for us is the argument of Ulpian in *D*.4.4.9.4 (book 11 on the *Edict*):

> Papinian says that if someone between the ages of twenty and twenty-five allows himself to be sold into slavery, that is, if he has shared in the price, restitution is generally not granted. This is correct, since a matter does not allow restitution when there is a change of status.

Quite typically, the jurist gives a formal legalistic reason in the last sentence for his opinion rather than basing it on grounds of justice, morality, or utility. The Roman jurists were bound to their own conception of the system's internal legal logic. This is the more striking in this instance because not only did ethical and practical arguments lie to hand, but Ulpian's legalistic reason is false. He himself shows in *D.4.4.3.6* that when a minor gave himself into adoption[13] and thus underwent a change of status he could successfully request restitution.

Civil law might also be used to effect changes in the *ius gentium* rule that a child born to a free woman was free, to a slave woman a slave.[14]

> G.1.81. It follows from these principles that by the law of nations a slave is born to a slave woman and a free man, and on the other hand a free child is born to a free woman and a slave . . . 83. Yet we must consider whether any law or the equivalent of a law has not altered the rule of the law of nations in any case. 84. Thus, under the *senatus consultum Claudianum* a female Roman citizen who cohabited with another's slave with the owner's permission might by agreement remain free but give birth to a slave. But later the divine Hadrian,[15] moved by the unfairness of the case and the inelegance of the law, restored the rule of the law of nations so that when the woman herself remains free she gives birth to a free child. 85. [*Something has been omitted by the scribe*] . . . it was possible for free children to be born to a slave woman and a free man; for by this law[16] it is provided that if a man cohabited with another's slave woman whom he thought was free then if male children are born they are free, if female they belong to the mother's owner. But in this instance, too, the divine Vespasian,[17] moved by the inelegance of the law, restored the rule of the law of nations, so that in every case, even if male children are born, they are the slaves of the mother's owner. 86. But that part of the law remains in force that enacted that slaves are born to a free woman and another's male slave whom she knew to be a slave. Thus, only among those peoples who have no such statute does a child follow the mother's status by the law of nations, and is free on that account.

The basic rule, described as being of the law of nations, that makes the child's status depend on that of the mother is commonsensical—any general rule that placed weight on the status of the supposed father would give rise to endless problems of proof. For the rest, the provisions are self-explanatory but more sexist than is usual in Roman law. This is particularly true of the *senatus con-sultum Claudianum,* which dates from A.D. 52: even apart from questions of race, sex between a female Roman and another's male slave was heinous, whereas no taboo existed against sex between a male citizen and a female slave. Indeed, where the female citizen's cohabitation was against the wishes of the slave's owner and he gave notice to her three times and she did not desist, then she, too, was enslaved.[18] By an imperial rescript of A.D. 317, the third notice had to be served in the presence of seven Roman witnesses.[19] It will be observed that the ruling of Hadrian which Gaius seems so approving of in G.1.84 would have the effect of making more free women slaves, since this would be in the interest of the owner of the male slave, who otherwise would not become owner of the offspring. But at least the choice facing the woman would have been simpler. The senatus consultum Claudianum and the ruling of Hadrian, incidentally, reveal that the social gulf between slave and free citizen is not necessarily wide. The situation under consideration involves not casual sex but cohabitation of a female citizen with another's slave, and the situation is obviously not unthinkable. Likewise, the law whose name has been lost shows that a free citizen might well cohabit with a slave whom he thought to be free. The legal gulf between free and slave is enormous, but how narrow the distinction might be in the reality of Rome is shown by a figure who appears prominently in the legal texts (but who will not specifically be examined in this book): the free person who in good faith serves as a slave. Very many texts discuss complex issues, such as whether he can be possessed and the circumstances in which acquisitions or rights belong to him or his supposed master.[20] To return to the law of enslavement:

> G.1.91. Again, if any pregnant female citizen becomes a slave under the *senatus consultum Claudianum* because she continued cohabitation with another's slave against the owner's wishes and warning, many jurists draw a distinction and hold that if the child was conceived in a civil law marriage then she gives birth to a Roman citizen, but if the child were conceived in promiscuous intercourse he is born the slave of the person whose slave the mother has become.

Even in this case many jurists were willing to apply the old Roman principle—of which Rabelais makes so much fun—that a child conceived during marriage is conclusively presumed to be the husband's. This is so even where the married free mother is cohabiting with the slave. Another Roman principle, namely, that an unborn child is to be treated as born so far as this is to its advantage, but not for the advantage of others or to its detriment, may have its origins in this context: Thus:

> *P.S.*2.24.3. If a slave woman conceives, then is freed, again becomes a slave, and then gives birth, she gives birth to a free person: for such middle periods aid liberty and cannot harm it.

The immediately preceding text justifies rulings of this kind on the basis of *favor libertatis,* the doctrine that, when possible, a decision or interpretation should be given in favor of freedom.[21] But favor libertatis could not always be applied:

> D.1.5.15 (Tryphoninus, book 10 of *Disputations*). By last will Arescusa was ordered to be free if she gave birth to three children. At the first birth she bore one, at the second three offspring. The question is raised whether any, and if so which, of the children were free? This condition attached to freedom now is to operate for the woman. But one should not doubt that the last child is born free. For nature does not permit two infants to emerge from the mother's womb at the same time by the same push, in such a way that by the uncertain order of birth it does not appear which is born in slavery or in freedom. The fulfillment of the condition at the beginning of the birth brings it about that the last born emerges from a free woman.

The condition attached to Arescusa's manumission was no doubt intended to stimulate procreation on her part. Arescusa was to be free when she produced three slaves. Breeding had become the main source of slaves. We may suppose some friendly intention on the part of the master, but at the same time the callousness that slavery engenders in the free population is apparent. (We need not, however, presume that Arescusa would be separated from her children, since freed slaves often continued to live in the house of their former master.) The text is also particularly revealing of the attitude of the Roman jurists to slavery. The rules here are worked out with the same rigor and the same logic as they are in other parts of the law.

The statute whose name we have lost, which is treated by Gaius in G.1.85,86, also created exceptions to the ius gentium. Apparently it had at least two provisions: first, children born to a free woman from sex with a man whom she knew to be another's slave are to be slaves; second, children born from the cohabitation of a free man with a slave whom he thought was free are to be free if male, slaves if female. Certainly the rules are inelegant, and we can believe that it was on that account that Vespasian declared that the children, male and female alike, born of the free father and slave mother should be slaves. But the result is equitable only on one view of justice, and, as Gaius notes, Vespasian did not repeal the other provision of the law which created a legal anomaly.

Two other anomalous instances, both of late Roman law, both introduced by emperors but to very different effect, should be discussed here. The emperor Justinian himself enacted in 531:

C.6.4.4.3. Likewise if anyone who does not have a wife at civil law, moved by love for his slave girl, makes her his concubine and remains in that intention until his death, but says nothing about her status, then not only does she herself become free and the children she conceived with her master, but they are even freeborn and moreover they benefit from their *peculia*. Nor do the heirs of the owner—whether they were his children or were outsiders—have patrons' rights over them.

A concubine had a semiofficial status in Roman law; she was a woman who lived in an open sexual relationship with a man who had neither a wife nor another concubine. Justinian, with extreme generosity (at another's expense), declares that where a concubine is the slave of her lover and the relationship endures until the master's death, then she is to be free and so are her children by the master if he has said nothing about her status (i.e., in his will). Further, they are to become owners of their *peculium,* the fund that the master allowed a slave to use as if it were the slave's, though in reality it was the master's (since a slave could own nothing). More extreme still—and indeed impossible, except that law can declare anything to be what it is not—the constitution enacts that the children (who were born slaves) are freeborn. Such laws reversing the truth are not uncommon at Rome.[22] The English scholar Buckland suggests that here the gift of freedom is retrospective, in

13

which case the fact that the children are freeborn would not be exceptional, but this interpretation is not favored by the wording of the constitution.[23]

The other anomalous instance is due to the emperor Anthemius in A.D. 468.

Novellae Anthemiae, 1.3. With regard to these women who enter into marriage vows with their own freedmen, we enact by this law which will last forever that such a forbidden conjunction may not even bear the name of marriage, but that women who execrably aspire to such illicit unions be punished by confiscation of all their property and by perpetual deportation. Those who are born from such an association are to be deprived not only of the right but even of the name of free men[24] and they shall rightly be assigned to a condition of slavery, so that our imperial treasury takes ownership of them.

The provisions of this law did not survive into Justinian's codification, where such a marriage was treated as indecorous but valid and not to be punished.[25] Not only is the tone of the law intemperate, but the law contains an extreme instance of punishment of children for the sins of a parent. It also contrasts greatly with a classical rule (which we will examine later) that a slave, freed by her master for the purpose of marriage with him, may not refuse the marriage.

If we take together [26] the rules that we have looked at relating to the legal consequences of sex between free and slave, we may see a pattern. The rules are not hostile to the sexual act in general, or C.6.4.4.3 could not have declared concubines free. For the same reason, among others, they are not directly against a sexual relationship between slaves and free. Nor is the function to discourage interference with other households, for then the male offspring of a free man and another's slave would not have been free. Equally, the purpose is not to restrain exploitation—mutual or not—of master and slave, as C.6.4.4.3 demonstrates. What does emerge is that a free man is not legally injured by a sexual relationship with a slave woman, and neither is the woman, and some of their children may be free, contrary to the law of nations; and yet a free woman may be legally injured by a relationship with a slave (or even with her own freedman), and, contrary to the law of nations, her children may be slaves. The explanation can only be that this is one form of that variety of sexism that regards a sexual relationship between a woman and a man of lower status as degrading to the woman, whereas a relationship between a man and a woman of lower status does not degrade the man.[27]

The above conclusion follows from the evidence on enslavement but is supported by a text that strictly speaking belongs in a different context, yet needs to be dealt with here:

> *C.Th.*9.9.1 (Constantine, A.D. 329). If any woman is discovered to have a secret sexual affair with her own slave, she shall be subjected to the capital sentence, and the rascal will be delivered to the fire. All persons will have permission to bring this public charge, and the power to report it is a duty. Even a slave is permitted to lodge a complaint and he is given his freedom if the charge is proved; but punishment hangs over him if the accusation is false. 1. A woman so married before the statute will be separated from such a union and will be deprived of the communion of the province and will mourn the absence of her exiled lover. 2. The children, too, whom she had from this union will be stripped of all insignia of rank and remain in bare liberty, and neither directly nor through the interposition of another person will they receive anything under any title of a will from the property of the woman. 3. But the succession to the woman on intestacy will be given to children, if there are any legitimate, or to the nearest kin or cognates or to that person whom the law admits, in such a way that whatever her lover or children by him had in any way in their own substance is joined to the property of the woman and is vindicated by her heirs just mentioned. 4 . . . 5 . . . 6 . . .

The sections of the rescript which are not quoted here extend the applications of the law to the case where only one of the lovers is alive at the passing of the law, but spare the offspring and prefer them for succession to brothers and remoter relations of the woman if both lovers have died. The part of the rescript that is quoted reappears with minor variations in Justinian's *Code,* 9.11.1. A striking feature of the opening part of the rescript is that this is one of the very few cases where a slave is allowed to give testimony against his owner. Here he is not only encouraged to do so but is given the enormous boon of liberty, a sign of the great official distaste for sex between a slave and his female owner. It may be worth mentioning that at no time was there a Roman rule prohibiting or even hindering interracial marriage or sex.

There were other civil law means of enslavement, most of which are important more for what they reveal of Roman attitudes than for their number. Possibly the most frequent case for early law was that of a *fur manifestus,* a thief caught in the act.[28]

> G.3.189. By the law of the Twelve Tables the penalty for manifest theft was capital. A free man was scourged and then solemnly assigned to the person from whom he had stolen. The old jurists debated whether by the assignment he became a slave or was in the position of a judgement debtor. A slave, after being similarly scourged, was put to death. But later the severity of the penalty was objected to, and an action for fourfold was established by the praetor's Edict both in the case of the free person and the slave.

The Twelve Tables are the famous legal code of the mid-fifth century B.C.; the mode of execution specified for slaves in this instance was to be thrown from the Tarpeian Rock.[29] The free man presumably was sold "across the Tiber,"[30] since it is said that a Roman could not become a slave at Rome (though we have just seen some exceptions). Judgement debtors (mentioned in the text of Gaius) could be put to death or sold "across the Tiber" after three market days if the debt was not paid. There is no evidence that this provision of the Twelve Tables was ever used. Similarly, in early law, a Roman who evaded military service, for instance by inflicting an injury on himself or by failing to enroll on the census, would be enslaved, presumably "across the Tiber." This practice also died out early, and one text suggests as the reason that there was no shortage of volunteers.[31] Deliberate failure to enroll in the census was itself a cause of enslavement, presumably because taxes on citizens were assessed from the census rolls. This rule lost all practical purpose around 166 B.C., after which the census was taken only very irregularly and at long intervals. Rome, because of its military conquests, had ceased to tax citizens.

In contrast, there is a late case of enslavement. In early and classical law if a child was exposed by his free father or by his owner, and the child was found and brought up by another, the child's status was unaffected; he remained, as he had been at birth,

free or a slave. But the Christian emperor Constantine enacted in
A.D. 331:

> *C.Th.*5.9.1. Whoever takes with him a boy or girl cast out of the father's
> home or with the wish and knowledge of the owner, and brings him up
> at his own expense, retains that person in the status he wished for him
> when he took him with him; that is, whether he preferred him to be a
> son or a slave. All anxiety must be thoroughly removed that those who
> knowingly and voluntarily cast out newborn infants whether slaves or
> free may recover them.

The practice of exposing infants was legally forbidden in 374, but
the law was obviously neglected, and Justinian enacted that exposed children retained their original status.[32]

Finally, we should look at reenslavement:

> J.1.16.1. The greatest change of status occurs when someone loses at the
> same time both citizenship and liberty. This happens to those who
> become slaves of punishment by the severity of the sentence[33] or to
> freedmen condemned for ingratitude to their patrons or to those who, in
> order to share in the price, allow themselves to be sold.

There seems to be no evidence for the Republic that ungrateful
freedmen could be reenslaved.[34] Claudius, who was emperor from
41 to 54, introduced reenslavement as the penalty for freedmen
who caused accusers to dispute the patron's status;[35] and in 56 a
movement in the senate to have reenslavement as a general penalty
available to the patron was blocked by Nero, who ruled that each
case was to be considered on its merits, though reenslavement was
one possible penalty.[36] The general rule was established by Commodus, emperor from 180 to 192:

> D.25.3.6.1 (Modestinus, sole book on *Manumissions*). This is the word-
> ing of the constitution of the Emperor Commodus: "When it is proved
> that patrons are violated by the insults of their freedmen or are struck by
> a vilely raised hand or even are abandoned when they are laboring under
> poverty or illness, then first the freedmen are to be reduced to the power
> of their patrons and forced to perform services for their masters. But if
> they do not accept this warning, then they may be awarded to a
> purchaser by the governor and the price paid to the patrons."

The power of reenslavement thereafter continued; it appears in
several texts of Justinian's *Code,*[37] and in the *Digest.*[38] Since such an

accusation was, in the Roman sense, a capital trial (i.e., it involved the greatest change of status, from citizen to slave), it was treated very seriously. The Roman jurists' dedication to the working out of detail is very evident in the texts relating to the patron's right to sue. Thus,

> *D.*40.9.30 (Ulpian, book 4 on the *Lex Aelia Sentia*). If anyone bought a slave under the express condition that he free him, and does not manumit him, and the slave then obtained his freedom under the constitution of the divine Marcus, the question may be asked whether the buyer can accuse him for ingratitude? And it may be said that since he did not manumit him the buyer does not have this right. 1. If my son manumitted a slave in accordance with my intention it may be doubted whether I have the right of accusation precisely because I did not manumit. But in fact I am to be regarded as if I had manumitted. 2. But if my son manumits a slave forming part of his *peculium castrense,* there is no doubt I will not have this right because I did not manumit. It is clear my son will be able to accuse. 3. A person can accuse so long as he remains patron. 4. Let us see whether, when patrons wish to accuse a freedman, the agreement of all is necessary or whether one can accuse? The better opinion is, if the freedman behaved badly to one patron, that patron can accuse him for ingratitude; but the agreement of all is needed if they are in the same position. 5. If a father assigned a freedman to one of his sons, Julian writes that he alone can accuse, for he alone is patron.

With regard to fr. 2, by the time of Ulpian in the late second century A.D., the *peculium castrense* (which was property gained by a son from military service) was, for most practical purposes, treated as if it belonged to the son. For fr. 5, a father by will had given his patron's rights to one of his sons.

> *C.*6.7.1. (Caracalla, A.D. 214). It is established that a person who manumitted on account of a trust cannot accuse for ingratitude, since that action is provided outside of the usual course of actions to a person who, by his own volition, gives freedom gratuitously, not to one who fulfills a debt.

> *C.*6.3.8 (Alexander Severus, A.D. 224). If the person who manumitted you had bought you with your own money, you do not owe him your days of work, nor can you be punished by him for ingratitude. Still, you ought not to deny that he is your patron.

This last text illustrates the democratic working of the rescript system, since it is addressed to a freedman called Augustinus who had given money from his peculium to an outsider who was to buy him and then free him.

> D.37.15.3 (Marcellus, sole book of *Replies*). Titius bought a slave and after many years ordered his sale. Then, begged by the slave, he freed him at the price of money accepted from him. I raise the question whether the son and heir of the manumitter can accuse him for ingratitude. He replied that the heir could if there was no other obstacle. It makes a great deal of difference whether one gives liberty for money accepted from one's own slave or his friend, or from that slave who, when he was another's, was transferred to you on trust. For in the former case the master conferred a benefit, even if not gratuitously; in the latter he did nothing but lend his services.

Though the decision in this text may at first sight seem out of harmony with those in the other texts quoted, the principle involved is the same. It was common for a master to allow his slave to buy his freedom when he had saved up enough money to do so, but this is treated as a benefit conferred by the master, since he is under no compulsion, morally or legally, to recognize the slave's right to the money (which technically, as we shall see, belongs to the master) or, even if he does, to give him his freedom in return. The situation is different if the slave had been transferred to the owner by will under the trust (*fideicommissum*) that he free him, or if the slave had provided money to someone not his owner with which to buy him and then release him, and the recipient did so.

To this point nothing has been said about enslavement by capture, the original important cause of slavery in the late Republic. This corresponds to its insignificance in the legal texts. Very few legal texts mention enslavement by capture, and those that do are mainly concerned with the capture of Romans by another people. Logically, Romans in that situation became slaves of the enemy. But some texts throw incidental light on the Roman law of slavery:

> D.49.15.5.2 (Pomponius, book 37 on *Quintus Mucius*). The right of return is also given in peace. For if we have neither friendship nor official ties of hospitality nor a treaty made for the sake of friendship with some people, although they are not enemies yet what of ours comes to them

> becomes theirs, and a free man of ours captured by them becomes theirs. The same is the case if something comes from them to us. In that case too the right of return is given.

The main thrust of the text concerns postliminium (the right of return) if either property belonging to a Roman or a free Roman citizen is captured. Where the Romans are the captors, the text mentions only property. But it is plausible that the same conditions apply where a free foreigner is captured by the Romans.[39] Then the clear implication of the text is that even in time of peace a person captured by the Romans becomes a slave if he belonged to a people that had neither official ties of hospitality nor a treaty made on account of friendship with the Romans. Of course, the capture is not by an individual Roman—that would be piracy or robbery[40]—but by the Roman state, and the newly made slave would become the property of the state. To become the property of an individual, the slave would have to be sold or given to him. One other text, Livy, *History of Rome,* 41.9.11, throws light on the issue. It concerns a temporary measure introduced by a senatus consultum of 177 B.C. stating that on manumission an oath had to be given that the manumission was not made to effect a change of citizenship. This was intended to stop Latins who wanted Roman citizenship from becoming slaves of Romans in order to be freed and hence become citizens. The text indicates that at that time Latins could become Roman slaves, but it does not show that they could be seized as captives since, presumably, they gave themselves into slavery.

The dearth of texts on enslavement by capture is to be explained by the absence of law. There were virtually no restrictions. Enslavement by capture was not limited to persons of a particular faith, from a particular place, or of a particular ethnic group.

Fully in keeping with their attitude toward enslavement and slavery, the Romans accept in a matter of fact way that Romans who are captured become slaves of their captors. As the text last quoted shows, for this to occur the captors need not be in a state of war with the Romans: it is enough that between the states there is no treaty of friendship or official ties of hospitality. The capture must be as the result of "official" hostility, not just criminality:

D.49.15.19.2 (Paul, book 16 on *Sabinus*). Persons captured by pirates and brigands continue to be free men.

A Roman so captured ceased to be a legal person.

D.49.15.18 (Ulpian, book 35 on *Sabinus*). In every branch of the law a person who fails to return from enemy hands is regarded as having died at the moment when he was captured.

A *lex Cornelia,* probably of around 84 to 81 B.C., ordered the execution of a will of a citizen who died a captive as if he had died at the moment of capture.[41] There was, of course, always the possibility that a captured Roman might return, and if he did so and if his capture and release were without loss of honor, then he might recover his former status by postliminium. This branch of the law was highly complex, sophisticated, and developed, even at an early date;[42] the prisoner's rights during his captivity and on his return varied according to the subject. Thus, to take marriage as an example:

D.49.15.12.4 (Tryphoninus, book 4 of *Disputations*). But the wife of a captive, however much she may wish it and although she may live in his house, is not married.[43]

Nor did marriage revive on his return; it only revived if the couple remarried.[44] There were two exceptional cases. First, if two Romans were captives and had a child and returned together, they were retroactively regarded as having been married, and the child was legitimate and in the power of the father.[45] This did not occur if they did not return together:

D.49.15.25 (Marcian, book 14 of *Institutes*). The deified Severus and Antoninus wrote in a rescript that if a wife was captured by the enemy along with her husband and there gave birth by her husband, if they returned they were legally parents and children and their child was in the father's power, insofar as he had returned with the right of *postliminium;* but if the child were to return with his mother alone he will be held a bastard, as if he were born without her having a husband.

Regarding the second exceptional case there was a dispute among jurists:

D.23.2.45.6 (Ulpian, book 3 on the *lex Iulia et Papia*). In the case of a woman whose patron has been captured by the enemy, I am inclined to think that she has the right to marry, just as she could if he were dead. But those who take Julian's view say that she does not have the right to marry, because according to Julian, a freedwoman's marriage continues even when her patron is in captivity, because of the respect she owes him. It is clear, however, that if the patron is enslaved in any other way, the marriage is undoubtedly dissolved.

Thus, Julian seems to have regarded marriage of a freedwoman with her patron to continue even during the latter's captivity. The explanation probably is that for Julian a freedwoman did not have the right to divorce her patron.[46]

We need not dwell here on other aspects of postliminium. But, for instance, in contrast to marriage, the paternal power over children was in an uncertain state: if the father died in captivity, the children were regarded as having become free from paternal power at the moment of his capture; if he returned they were regarded as having always been in his power.[47]

Two

Manumission and Citizenship

R oman slavery, viewed as a legal institution, makes sense on the assumption that slaves could reasonably aspire to being freed and hence to becoming Roman citizens or, at least, that the main rules of the institution were framed with those slaves primarily in mind who could reasonably have such an aspiration. And we know from various sources that both in the late Republic and in the early Empire there were tens of thousands of ex-slaves mingling with the freeborn inside the city of Rome itself.[1] Epigraphical evidence indicates that domestic slaves were often manumitted around the age of thirty, and a speech of Cicero tells us in effect that six years was a longer period than careful, hardworking slaves who had been captured in war should expect to serve.[2] Still, in fact, the great bulk of slaves, especially those who were engaged in menial, non-domestic tasks, probably had no realistic hope of changing their status. Typically, as in this instance, legal rules regulate a variety of situations.

Three methods of manumission are usually regarded as classical in the sense that they are mentioned by Gaius, are alone mentioned by Gaius as proper modes of manumission, and give citizenship as well as freedom.

G.1.17. He becomes a Roman citizen in whom these three elements concur: he is over thirty years old; he was held by his owner in full Roman ownership; and is freed by a statutorily recognized mode of manumission, that is, by *vindicta,* by the census, or by testament. But if any of these elements are lacking, he will become a Latin.

The status of Latinity for improperly manumitted slaves will be discussed later in this chapter.

These three methods of manumission all existed as early as the Twelve Tables, though that code, so far as we can tell, mentioned only manumission by will.

Manumission by census was the enrollment of a slave, with his owner's consent, on the census list of Roman citizens. Since the census was so formal and was taken only once every five years, this mode of manumission is unlikely to have arisen if manumission *vindicta* with the full effect of giving citizenship had already existed. According to tradition, the sixth king of Rome, Servius Tullius (578–535), allowed slaves who had been manumitted but who wished not to return to their old country to enroll themselves on the census and become citizens. Hence an earlier form of manumission had not given citizenship, and it was precisely the acquisition of citizenship which was the object of this reform. It is noteworthy, then, that some activity of the state was needed for the acquisition of citizenship. What is not clear for this form of manumission, and is disputed,[3] is whether the censor openly declared he was giving citizenship to the (now ex-) slave or whether he operated under the fiction that the enrolled citizen had always been a citizen. As we saw in the previous chapter, the taking of the census was largely abandoned after 166 B.C., and with it, despite Gaius, would disappear manumission by enrollment in the census. In fact, this mode of manumission is likely to have become rare as soon as manumission vindicta gave citizenship.[4]

Manumission vindicta is a juristic dodge, a particular fictional use of the *vindicatio in libertatem,* "the claim for freedom," which was brought when a free man was wrongfully held as a slave. For this application of the action, the master who wished to free his slave arranged for a friend to bring the claim against him in front of the magistrate; the master put up no defense, and the magistrate declared the slave free. The cooperation of the magistrate is obviously needed for the dodge to work.[5] Citizenship was also acquired by this mode of manumission, but perhaps not originally. In fact, there is a legal legend—certainly not straight history—reported by Livy, *History of Rome,* 2.3 ff, relating to 509 B.C., the first year of the Republic. A slave, Vindicius, informed the consuls of a conspiracy to restore the Monarchy, and he was manumitted vindicta. Apocryphal although the story is,[6] it seems intended to explain why the private act of the master has public consequences for a slave— namely, the acquisition of citizenship.[7]

Manumission vindicta and perhaps also manumission by the census operated on the false basis that the slave was a free man— with manumission vindicta there was even the appearance of a free man's having been wrongfully held as a slave—and yet the law recognized the true state of affairs and gave to the former master the full rights of a patron.[8] This ability not to extend conclusions to the point of absurdity is typical of Roman law.

Very different is manumission by testament, which did not involve any dodge, though it conferred citizenship, and which, alone of the three, could be conditional. Naturally only a slave belonging to the testator could be given freedom directly by testament. A slave to whom freedom is given conditionally by will is called a *statuliber* until the condition is realized. The status was recognized by the Twelve Tables:

> *Epitome Ulpiani,* 2.4. A slave, ordered to be free under this condition "if he gives ten thousand to my heir," even if he be alienated by the heir will achieve freedom by giving the money to the purchaser. The Twelve Tables order this.[9]

Actually, at the time of the Twelve Tables, Rome had a precoinage culture. The example in the text is therefore anachronistic, and the word *emptor,* translated here properly as "purchaser," had originally the wider sense of "taker." The status of the statuliber is so special that it will be treated separately at the end of this chapter.

At the time of the Twelve Tables there were two forms of making wills, *testamentum calatis comitiis* and *testamentum per aes et libram;* the latter represented an existing practice that was in effect ratified by the code. Since manumission by will was, as we have seen, clearly established by the time of the Twelve Tables and needed no ratification, it must originally have been possible only by a testamentum calatis comitiis.[10] Later it was standard in the testamentum per aes et libram (and in fact the will calatis comitiis did not long survive). The point is important for the history of manumission because of a vital difference between the two forms of wills. The former had to be made publicly in the assembly called the *comitia calata,* it required the express approval of the members, and it was actually and technically an act of legislation. The latter was a personal and private act. Thus, originally in this form of manumission, too, the conferring of freedom and citizenship required the participation and approval of the state.

For the manumission to take effect, the intention of the testator had to be clear and the gift of liberty had to be expressed in imperative words. The *lex Fufia Caninia* of 2 B.C. required that the slave to be freed be expressly named:

> G.2.239. Likewise freedom, it seems, cannot be given to an uncertain person, since the *lex Fufia Caninia* orders slaves to be freed by name.[11]

There could not, generally speaking, be an implied gift of freedom, even though there was a general principle expressed by Paul in *D.50.17.17a* (book 16 on *Plautius*):

> When the intention of the manumitter is obscure, liberty is to be favored.

We find texts such as the following:

> D.40.4.2 (Ulpian, book 5 on *Sabinus*). If anyone institutes the heir thus: "Let Titius be my heir. If Titius will not be my heir, let Stichus be my heir. Let Stichus be free." Then according to Aristo, if Titius is heir, Stichus is not free. To me it seems he can be said to be free as if he had not received freedom in any one grade but in two. And this is the law in force.

By "in two," *dupliciter,* Ulpian means that the grant is to be regarded as if it had been written out twice, once for each hypothesis. The wording of the testament does appear to be ambiguous, and whether the testator wished Stichus to be free if Titius was heir is not clear. This would therefore seem to be a case for favor libertatis, but there is no sign of that in Aristo's decision. Ulpian's very different approach is to hold that in both hypotheses there was an express clause of manumission. Recognition of an implied gift of freedom just does not appear in the text. Such recognition, however, was accepted in two situations by the time of Justinian:

C.6.27.5.1 (Justinian, A.D. 531). There was matter for doubt where a testator appointed his slave his heir but without mentioning freedom; and this raised such contention among the old jurists that it is scarce possible to see that it was decided. 1a. But this altercation is to be left to antiquity. We have found another method of reaching a decision, since we always follow the traces of the intention of testators. 1b. When we therefore find introduced by our law that if anyone appoints his own slave as tutor to his sons and does not mention liberty, liberty is also presumed to have been granted by the very appointment as tutor so as to favor the pupils; then if anyone appoints his own slave as heir without mentioning freedom, surely he always becomes a Roman citizen?

Justinian's rhetorical question is possibly out of place, because slaves, peregrines, and even Junian Latins could not be tutors. Hence, if the testator wished the appointment of his slave as tutor to be valid, he had to have intended the slave to be free and a citizen. It is easy to imply the gift of freedom here, especially for the reason expressed by Justinian, "to favor the pupils," that is, the freeborn children of the testator who are still under the age of puberty. The case of one's own slave appointed as heir is very different, and the argument for liberty would be something else. The Roman rule was that no one could die partly testate. Hence, if the slave was heir and took the inheritance by will, he himself could not be the slave of the person who would be heir on intestacy. Unless he were free, he would be a slave, but the slave of no one. Hence, his institution as heir also implied a gift of liberty. But the argument from the one case to the other is not straightforward.

In the Republic there was another form of manumission, which does not seem to have survived into the Empire, namely, where the master adopted his slave as his child or gave the slave in adoption to another.[12] The act of adoption gave automatic manumission. Justinian, to some extent, restored the practice: a master who declared in writing that his slave was his son thereby made him free, but the writing was not sufficient to confer the rights of a son on the ex-slave.

From a text of Cicero we know that in the late Republic informal manumission did not give freedom.[13] The position was regularized by a *lex Junia* whose date is uncertain but which is almost certainly of the reign of Augustus:

> G.3.56. To make this branch of the law clearer we must remember what I have said elsewhere, that those who are now called Junian Latins were at an earlier time slaves by the law of Roman citizens, but were maintained in apparent freedom by the aid of the praetor; and hence their property used to pass (i.e., on death) to their patrons by title of *peculium*. Later by the *lex Junia* all those whom the praetor protected in a state of liberty became free and were called Junian Latins: Latins, because the state made them free as if they were freeborn Roman citizens who, by migrating from the city of Rome into Latin colonies, had become colonial Latins; Junian, because they became free by the *lex Junia* even though they were not Roman citizens.[14]

The continuation of the text and others which describe the condition of Junian Latins will be discussed later. Thus, for some time before the lex Junia, the praetor had intervened to give protection, obviously against actual reenslavement, to a slave manumitted informally or when some other necessary condition was lacking for fully valid manumission. The reign of Augustus also saw two other fundamental statutes in the history of Roman slavery. The earlier was the lex Fufia Caninia of 2 B.C., which is explained by Gaius:

> G.1.42. Moreover, by the *lex Fufia Caninia,* a limitation has been set on the manumission of slaves by will. 43. For a master who has more than two and not more than ten slaves is permitted to manumit up to one-half; he who has more than ten and not more than thirty is permitted to manumit up to one-third of that number; he who has more than thirty but not more than one hundred has the power of manu-mitting one-quarter; finally, he who has more than one hundred and not more than five hundred is not permitted to manumit more than one-fifth; nor is power given to manumit more to a person who has more than five hundred, for the law provides that no one may manumit more than one hundred. But if a person has only one or even two slaves he is not affected by this law and so he has full freedom of manumission.[15]

The provision tells its own story. Since it envisages that a Roman might have more than five hundred slaves, slaves were obviously extremely numerous.[16] Freedmen must also have become very common, since the point of the provision is to restrict their numbers, and limitations up to one hundred are imposed on manumissions by will. The provision applied only to manumissions by will,[17] hence the damage to be feared occurred only or predominantly in this case. We can assume that most manumissions would be by testament, since that would not deprive the master of the slaves' services during his lifetime and he would have, as the ancient moralists put it, grateful freedmen to attend his funeral. Finally, the provision betrays anxiety about the numbers of freedmen at Rome, yet the limitations are not obviously ungenerous. The provision does not limit manumissions by reference to racial origin or to the qualifications of the slaves. To prevent fraud, the lex Fufia Caninia also provided that the slaves to be manumitted had to be expressly named.

The second relevant Augustan statute was the *lex Aelia Sentia* of A.D. 4, which contained various provisions:

G.1.18. The requirement relating to the slave's age was introduced by the *lex Aelia Sentia*. For that statute decreed that slaves manumitted under the age of thirty did not become citizens unless they were freed *vindicta* after proof of a just cause of manumission in front of the *consilium* (council). There is a just cause of manumission, for instance, if a person manumits before the *consilium* his natural son or daughter or natural brother or sister or his foster child or teacher, or a slave whom he wants to have as his general agent or a slave woman whom he wants to marry.[18]

G.1.37. If a person manumits in fraud of creditors or in fraud of his patron he achieves nothing, because the *lex Aelia Sentia* prohibits freedom. 38. Similarly, by the same law a master under twenty is not permitted to manumit except *vindicta* and with good cause for manumission shown before a council. 39. There is good reason for manumission if anyone manumits his father or mother or teacher or foster-brother. Moreover, the reasons I have set out above for a slave under thirty can be adduced also in the present case. Conversely, the reasons I have produced with regard to an owner under twenty can also be applied to a slave under thirty. 40. Since therefore a limitation on manumission was established by the *lex Aelia Sentia* for masters under twenty, it happens that those who have reached the age of fourteen, although they can make a will and in it appoint an heir or leave legacies, nonetheless if they are under the age of twenty cannot give freedom to a slave. 41. Though the owner under twenty wishes to make the slave a Latin, he must nonetheless show adequate reason before the *consilium* and only then free him before friends (i.e., informally).

G.1.13. It is provided by the *lex Aelia Sentia* that slaves who were put in bonds by their master by way of punishment or have been branded or have been questioned under torture for wrongdoing and found guilty or have been handed over to fight in the arena with men or beasts or have been thrown into a gladiatorial school prison, and then were manumitted by the same or another master, are free men of the status of surrendered enemies. Slaves who have been so disgraced never become Roman citizens or Latins, however they are manumitted and whatever their age, even if they were in the full ownership of their masters. They are always ranked as surrendered enemies.

Persons classed as *peregrini dediticii,* "surrendered enemies (or foreigners)" had the further disability that they were sold into slavery with their goods if they attempted to settle within one hundred miles of Rome. One significant detail in G.1.13 (which appears also in *Epit. Ulp.* 1.11) should be noted. The lex Aelia Sentia's provision on slaves punished by their master takes no account of the guilt or innocence of the slave. To prevent manumission conferring citizenship, it is enough and solely relevant that the slave was bound by the master. It is only for public trials that the slave's guilt has to be established before citizenship is inhibited. There is thus to be no investigation into the justice of the master's treatment of his slave.

None of these restrictions on manumission under the lex Aelia Sentia applied if the owner was insolvent and freed the slave whom he appointed heir by will, and there was no other heir.[19] The reason for the exception is that it was the slave (who could not refuse the inheritance) and not the dead owner who suffered the disgrace of bankruptcy.

Informal manumission, as we have seen, conferred Junian Latinity, but the only effective modes of informal manumission were *per epistulam,* by a letter conferring freedom, and *inter amicos,* which involved a declaration made before friends (or witnesses). Late texts mention informal manumission at a feast (*in convivio*),[20] but this may simply be a variation of manumission inter amicos.

When the Empire became Christian, a new mode of manumission, *in ecclesia* (in church), was regulated by Constantine, the first Christian emperor. A rescript of 310 declares that it is long settled that a master can free his slave in church, but the manumission has to be before the people, in the presence of the priests, and there must be a writing signed by the owner.[21] The rescript apparently did not give the slave citizenship, but this defect was remedied by another rescript five years later.[22] Henceforward this should be regarded as a formal mode of manumission.[23]

But a slave who, on manumission, became only a Latin might become a Roman citizen in various ways:

> G.1.29. To begin with, under the *lex Aelia Sentia,* slaves who are manumitted under thirty and have become Latins, if they take wives who are Roman citizens or colonial Latins or of his own status, and this is attested by not less than seven witnesses who are Roman citizens above puberty, and they beget a son, when this son becomes one year old, the power is given to them to go before the praetor or, in a province, before the governor and prove that he married a wife under the *lex Aelia Sentia* and from her has a one-year-old son. And if the magistrate before whom the case is proved so pronounces, then both the Latin himself and his wife if she too be of the same status, and also the son if he be of the same condition, are ordered by the statute to be Roman citizens.

Not only does this text indicate an absence of any repugnance to the notion that ex-slaves can become Roman citizens, but, since the statute offered an inducement to ex-slaves to procreate, it also indicates a positive desire to welcome the progeny of such into the state. The statute also applied if the child was a daughter and even if the father died before the child became one year old.[24] The *lex Visellia* of A.D. 23 gave citizenship to those who were Latins by manumission and who served six years in the police at Rome. A decree of the senate reduced the period of service to three years.[25] Ex-slaves obviously were thought to include responsible and respectable men. Again, the emperor Claudius declared that Latins became Roman who built a seagoing ship holding at least ten thousand measures of corn, and the ship (or a substitute) carried corn to Rome for six years.[26] Nero enacted that a Latin whose fortune was at least two hundred thousand sesterces and who built in Rome a house on which he spent at least half of his fortune was to become a Roman.[27] Trajan declared that a Latin who operated a mill in the city for three years and the mill ground not less than one hundred measures of corn daily was to become a citizen.[28] Freedmen, obviously, could be wealthy. Significantly, some of these methods of attaining citizenship were restricted to those ex-slaves who remained in Rome.

It remains to mention, for classical law, manumission by a person who had effective ownership—who had the slave *in bonis*—but not full civil law ownership:

> G.1.35. Thus, if a slave is yours by bonitary ownership and mine by full civil law, he can be made a Latin by you acting alone, but a repeated manumission can be made by me—and not by you—and in this way, he becomes my freedman.[29]

A Roman would have bonitary ownership, have the slave in bonis, if the slave had been delivered to him by the owner without the necessary formalities to effect transfer of ownership. The full civil law owner could not recover his slave. The period of prescription which would give the bonitary owner full civil law ownership was one year. The one situation where in practice there was a real difference between bonitary and full Roman ownership is here: a bonitary owner could not manumit a slave so as to give him Roman citizenship.

The law in the time of Justinian—which, of course, is that relevant for later history—was subject to various changes. One change that affected slavery, though that was not the end in view, was the abolition of the distinction between full civil law ownership and bonitary ownership.[30] Those who formerly had bonitary ownership were now full owners. More directly related to slavery was the very early repeal (in 528) of the lex Fufia Caninia:

> J.1.7.1. By the *lex Fufia Caninia* a limitation was imposed on manumitting slaves by will. We decided that this must be revoked as an impediment to freedom and something insidious; it was inhuman that the living could grant freedom to all their household (unless some other

cause obstructed freedom) but that the same license should be taken away from the dying.[31]

Two years later came the repeal of the *senatus consultum Claudianum.*

> J.3.12.1. There was also a wretched universal succession under the *senatus consultum Claudianum* when a free woman mad with love for a slave would lose her liberty under the *senatus consultum,* and, with her liberty, her property. We believed this to be unworthy of our times and hence allowed it to be abolished in our state and not to be inserted in our *Digest.*

Further reforms are recorded in J.1.5.3:

> Formerly there was a threefold status for freedmen: those who were manumitted might acquire full legal freedom and become Roman citizens; or a lesser grade and become Latins under the *lex Junia Norbana;* or a still lower grade and be classed as surrendered enemies under the *lex Aelia Sentia.* But this wretched status of surrendered enemies had long been obsolete,[32] and that of Latins was not common. Therefore in our piety, wishing to improve all things and produce a better situation, we changed this by two constitutions and restored things to their pristine state since from the earliest days of the city of Rome only one straightforward freedom existed, namely, the same that the manumitter had, except that the person freed is a freedman, although the manumitter is freeborn. We abolished the status of surrendered enemies by a constitution[33] that we promulgated among our decisions whereby, on the advice of that exalted man, our quaestor Tribonian, we settled the disputes of old law. At the suggestion of the same quaestor, by another constitution,[34] which shines out among imperial laws, we abolished Junian Latinity and everything connected with it, and, as was once the law, granted Roman citizenship to all freedmen, with no distinction drawn as to the age of the person manumitted or of the owner manumitting, or as to the mode of manumission. We also added many ways by which slaves may achieve freedom, along with that Roman citizenship which alone exists today.

The decisions referred to in the text would seem to be the collection known as the Fifty Decisions which was issued in 530 or early 531 to resolve longstanding and unsettled disputes of the classical jurists. The collection itself has not survived, and not all of the constitutions can be traced. In a long and complicated constitution of the year 531 (*C.*7.6a.), Justinian regulated informal manumission. Only certain modes of informal manumission had any effect, but these were now all to confer citizenship. Two of these modes were to require witnesses—namely, per epistulam, which needed five witnesses writing their names on the letter in imitation of a codicil,[35] and inter amicos, which also needed five witnesses, the formal recording of the act by the master, and the evidence signed by the five witnesses and by a *tabellio* (who was, in effect, akin to a notary).[36] Slaves who, by order of the deceased or his heir, stood around the funeral couch or walked in the funeral procession wearing the cap of liberty (*pilleus*) were also to be free.[37] A slave woman whose master gave her in marriage to a free man and provided in writing a dowry became free[38]—dowry was an indication of marriage, and only free persons could marry. Again, a master's notification in the official records that his slave was his son bestowed freedom on the slave.[39] Finally, freedom was acquired when the master gave to the slave or destroyed, in the presence of witnesses, the papers that constituted evidence of the slavery.[40]

Something more must be said about the special position of the statuliberi, slaves who, under a pending condition in a will, are to be free. For the status to exist, the will had to be valid.[41] When the status did exist, it continued even if the statuliber was transferred by the heir or if, possessed in good faith by someone else, he was usucapted (that is, title to him was acquired by lapse of time).[42] To become free, the statuliber had to comply with the condition, but if he was prevented from complying by the heir or other successor in title, then he was automatically free.[43] The general tenor of the texts in the relevant *Digest* title (*D.*40.7) shows that the jurists were very protective of the rights of statuliberi.

Three

Freedmen, Patrons,
and the State

Roman citizenship, it should be understood, was a highly prized possession that conferred important rights and privileges on the holders. Hence it was jealously guarded, and hence, too, the revolt of Rome's Italian allies in 91–88 B.C., known as the Social War. The objective of the allies was to be granted citizenship.

Rome, in fact, was exceptionally generous in the ancient world (and in more recent times) in granting citizenship to freed slaves. This makes it important to ask why some masters, who could have freed formally, preferred to manumit informally and thus deprive the former slave of Roman citizenship. The answer, as we shall see, lies in the greater succession rights the former master of such a slave had. But first we shall consider the relationship between a patron and his former slave, now a citizen. The rights of a patron fall into three classes: rights of succession on the freedman's death; a right to *obsequium*, let us say "respect"; and a right to *operae*, a fixed number of days of work.[1]

A right of succession on intestacy was given by the Twelve Tables, but only later, by the Edict of the praetor, was a right given to a patron to succeed against the freedman's will.

G.3.40. Once it was permitted to a freedman to pass over his patron with impunity in his will. For the Law of the Twelve Tables called the patron to the inheritance of his freedman only if the freedman died intestate leaving no *suus heres.* And so also on the death, intestate, of a freedman, if he had left a *suus heres,* his patron had no rights to his property. Of course, if he had left as his *suus heres* one of his natural children, there was no grievance; but if the *suus heres* was an adopted son or daughter or wife *in manu,* then clearly it was unjust that no right remained for the patron. 41. Therefore, this legal injustice was later amended by the praetor's Edict. For if a freedman makes a will he is ordered to make it in such a way that he leaves his patron half of his property; and if he leaves him nothing or less than half, possession of the estate for half share is granted to the patron in defiance of the testament. If he dies intestate, leaving as his *suus heres* an adopted son or a wife whom he had *in manu,* or a daughter-in-law who had been *in manu* of his son, possession of the estate to a one-half share is equally given to the patron against these *sui heredes.* But natural children avail a freedman to exclude his patron, not only those whom he has in his power at the time of his death, but also those who are emancipated and given in adoption, provided they were named to some share of heirs or, if they were passed over in the will, they claimed possession of the estate in defiance of the will in accordance with the Edict. If they were disinherited they do not at all exclude the patron. 42. Later, by the *lex Papia,* the rights of patrons were increased so far as concerns wealthier freedman. For it is provided by that statute, that from the estate of one who leaves a fortune of more than one hundred thousand sesterces and has fewer than three children, whether he dies testate or intestate, an equal share is due to the patron. Thus, when the freedman leaves one son or one daughter as his heir, half of the property is due to the patron, just as if the freedman had died without any son or daughter; when the freedman leaves two sons or daughters as heirs, a third part is due; if he leaves three, the patron is excluded. 43. Under the old law patrons suffered no injustice with regard to the estates of freedwomen. For, since freedwomen were in the statutory guardianship of their patrons, they could not make a testament without the patron's approval. Hence, if he had given authority for the making of the will, he had only himself to blame if he was not left heir by her, or, if he were appointed heir, the inheritance came to him by testament. If he had not given authority and the freedwoman died intestate, the inheritance passed to him, since a woman cannot have a *suus heres.* In the old days there was no one, whether heir or possessor of the estate, who could exclude a patron from the estate of his intestate freedwomen. 44. But later the *lex Papia,* since by virtue of four children it freed freedwomen from the guardianship of their patrons and thus permitted them to make a testament even without the authority of a tutor, provided that for the number of children whom the freedwoman had at the time of her death an equal share would be due to the patron. Thus, from the estate of a woman who left four surviving children, a fifth share is due to the patron; but if she outlives all her children, the entire estate goes to the patron.[2]

This long quotation from Gaius requires some elucidation. Legally the most important domestic unit at Rome was the family under the control of its male head, the *paterfamilias*. The paterfamilias had *potestas*, "power," over his direct descendants born in a full Roman marriage and over grandchildren and descendants born in a full Roman marriage to his male descendants. Potestas could also be acquired by adoption. *Patria potestas* lasted until the father's death—no matter how old the descendants were—but it could be lost by emancipation, that is, if the parent voluntarily and in a formal ceremony gave up his potestas, or if the parent gave the descendant in adoption. Full Roman marriage was of two types, with *manus* or without manus. In the former, which was the usual in early times but rare by the Empire, the wife entered the manus of her husband (or his ascendant), another form of control which was very like potestas, and became a full member of the husband's family. In the latter, the wife did not enter the manus or power of her husband, but remained in the potestas of her father or remoter male ascendant if any such was alive; failing such an ancestor, the woman would have been and remained *sui iuris,* "independent." The paterfamilias was not, of course, in the potestas of anyone else and hence was also independent, sui iuris. More immediately to the text of Gaius, then, a *suus heres* was a member of a Roman family who became independent by the death: that is, sons and daughters of the deceased, whether adoptive or natural (provided they had not been emancipated or given in adoption), and, similarly, grandsons and granddaughters by a son who had predeceased, a wife *in manu,* and daughter-in-law in manu whose husband had predeceased. As to G.3.41, the praetorian Edict, following narrower rules of the civil law, required that, for a will to be enforceable all male descendants, not just sons, who were not appointed heirs had to be disinherited by name; a general clause of disinherison was

sufficient to exclude females. If such persons were simply passed
over without mention in the will, they could attack the testament
and in effect have it set aside. The relevant provisions applied to all
who would have been sui *heredes* had they not undergone a change
of family, except for adoptive children who had been emancipated
and for natural children who had been given in adoption and who
were still in their adoptive family.[3]

The *lex Papia Poppaea,* referred to in G.3.42 and 44, was enacted
in A.D. 9 under Augustus and formed, along with the *lex Julia de
maritandis ordinibus* of 18 B.C., a large corpus of rules relating to
marriage. It is not easy to disentangle the provisions of the statutes,
which are, in fact, often cited together by the Roman jurists as the
lex Julia et Papia, as if they comprised one statute. For us it is enough
to notice at this point that one main aim of the legislation was to
encourage marriage and procreation.[4] It is instructive to compare
the freedom from guardianship conferred by the statute upon
freedwomen with that granted to freeborn women:

> G.1.194. Freeborn women are released from guardianship by right of
> three <children, freedwomen by four> if they are in the statutory
> guardianship <of their patron> or his children; or, if they have tutors
> of another sort, such as fiduciary or Atilian,[5] then in right of three
> children.

(The words in brackets represent the standard reconstruction of a
supposed accidental omission in the manuscript.) Women who
were independent were under perpetual guardianship and required
the authority of their guardians for various transactions. This
guardianship was becoming unreal even before the time of Gaius,
but it remained significant in the case of *tutela legitima,* "statutory
guardianship," which for a freedwoman would be usual when she
was in the guardianship of her patron, for a freeborn woman when
no guardian had been appointed to her by testament and her
guardian (or guardians) was the nearest agnate (or agnates), in
accordance with the Twelve Tables. For the lex Papia Poppaea,
release from guardianship was obviously envisaged as an incentive
to increase the birth rate; and that one child more was required
from a freedwoman to end the statutory guardianship of the patron

is clearly a response to the feeling that a master who freed a slave should have greater rights than a brother or remoter agnate. The significant point is that under Augustus the procreation of children by freedwomen was officially encouraged. This may seem strange at first, in view of the provision of another Augustan statute, the lex Fufia Caninia of seven years earlier, which imposed restrictions on the manumission of slaves by will. If the two provisions do not conflict, then we must hold that the leading Romans of the time who were responsible for the legislation believed that it was socially objectionable to have at Rome large numbers of freed persons but not objectionable to have large numbers of freeborn children of freed persons.[6] If this conclusion is correct, then it must follow, first, that the objections to manumission was not based on any racial or nationalistic considerations, and, second, since a rise in the birth rate was being generally sought, that there was no objection on economic grounds to an increase in the Roman free population. This would then suggest that there was at least a strong suspicion that slavery was detrimental to the slave's character, that freedmen as a group—particularly those freed, perhaps rather indis-criminantly, by testament—were rather untrustworthy, but that the taint was not passed on to the children born in freedom to ex-slaves.

Gaius in 3.45–54 then goes on to list the succession rights to freed persons of the children and remoter descendants of a male or female patron. We need not enter upon the detail: it is sufficient that the succession rights of a patron did not by any means come to an end by his or her death.

The second right of the patron was to obsequium, respect. What is involved here is not easily stated—the Roman jurists, as usual, proffer no definition—but is elucidated by a number of specific rules. For instance, the praetor's Edict contained a clause (as reconstructed by Otto Lenel):[7]

> Let no one without my permission summon to court a parent, a male or female patron, or the children or parents of a male or female patron.[8]

If the praetor's consent was required before any action could be brought against the patron, then actions that brought descredit on a defendant who lost could not be brought at all:

C.6.6.1 (Alexander Severus, A.D. 223). Against your patron you may not institute an action that brings discredit.

This limitation was not restricted to the group of actions which brought *infamia,* a technical form of disgrace, on the unsuccessful defendant.[9] The fact that a freedman could not sue his patron for physical or verbal injury[10] should not be taken to mean that the patron had a legal right to punish his freedman—the otherwise appropriate action, the *actio iniuriarum,* was simply one that brought discredit on an unsuccessful defendant.[11] Similarly, a freedman could neither accuse nor give evidence against his patron in a criminal charge.[12] A gift made by a patron to a freedman could be revoked at any time, even without cause,[13] and the prohibition of gifts (except between specified groups) under the *lex Cincia* did not extend to gifts to the patron.[14] If a master voluntarily freed a slave woman specifically in order to marry her, she could not refuse; indeed, the lex Julia et Papia enacted in so many words: "Let a freedwoman who is married to her patron have no power to divorce."[15] Particular obligations arose when a patron was in need:

P.S.2.32. A freedman, free from the obligation of gifts, or gifts on special occasions and from days of labor, is compelled in accordance with his resources to support his needy patron.[16]

The obligation of obsequium due to a patron was also in some degree due to his parents and children.[17]

It should not be thought that the obligation of respect was all one way. Thus, the patron must not treat the freedman as a slave,[18] he could not give evidence in criminal cases against him in classical law, and, in late law, he could not be compelled to do so.[19] Again, gifts to a freedman from his patron were exempt from the restrictions of the lex Cincia,[20] and a patron who did not support his needy freedman lost his rights of patronage.[21] A patron could not prohibit his freedman from operating the same kind of business as his own in the district in which they both lived.[22] In a similar vein, another text, probably giving an answer to an actual question, reports that a freedwoman is not classed as ungrateful if she exercised her art contrary to the wishes of her female patron.[23] A freedman could not be forced to occupy the same house as his patron.[24]

The third right of the patron who freed voluntarily was to operae, days of work whose number was fixed by agreement, and such an agreement is thought to have been usual. By the terms of the relevant edict of the praetor, the agreement was not to be intended to operate as a burden on liberty.[25] Thus, the number of days work and their character had to be reasonable.

> D.38.1.16.1 (Paul, book 40 on the *Edict*). Such days of work are given to the patron as ought to be estimated in accordance with the age, dignity, health, needs, and other such factors, with regard to both parties.[26]

Immediately before, in the *principium* of the text, Paul wrote:

> A freedman should provide days of work of that trade or skill that he learnt after manumission, if they are of a kind that are provided honestly and without danger to life; nor are those always due that were bound to be provided at the time of manumission. But, if the freedman later engages in improper work, he is bound to provide days of labor such as he was producing at the time of manumission.

Similarly, on the basis of reasonableness, we find a text of Ulpian:

> D.38.1.15.pr. (book 38 on the *Edict*). After the imposition of days of work, a freedman who was prevented by ill health from providing them is not liable. For it cannot be regarded as his fault that he does not produce the work.

Again:

> D.38.1.46 (Valens, book 5 on *Trusts*). It is settled that an action for days of work should not be given against a freedwoman who lived in concubinage with her patron, just on the same basis as if she had been married to him.[27]

And a freedwoman who married another person with her patron's consent could not be sued for operae;[28] nor could one who reached the age of fifty.[29] But, significantly:

> D.38.1.48.2 (Hermogenianus, book 2 of the *Epitome of the Law*). The exaction of days of work is not denied to a female patron, nor to a male patron's daughter, granddaughter, and great-granddaughter who consented to the marriage of a freedwoman, because to such persons these work days are not given indecorously.

Marriage by itself did not release a freedman from operae,[30] but by
the *lex Julia de maritandis ordinibus,* having two children in power
did.

> C.6.3.7.1 (Alexander Severus, A.D. 224). A person who had two children
> in his power, even at different times, is freed from the obligation of days
> of work by the *lex Julia de maritandis ordinibus.*

The requirement that the person released had the children in power
shows that the provision related to a freedman who had contracted
a full Roman marriage.

The patron's rights to operae would also be lost on account of his
improper behavior, for instance, if he sought to reenslave the
freedman[31] or exacted an oath not to marry or bring up children.[32]

When the freedman became a Latin and not a Roman citizen, the
patron's rights of succession were much greater. Until the lex Junia,
slaves freed informally remained, as we have seen, slaves, but the
praetor saw to it that they received protection from their masters.
But, of course, they died as slaves, and their whole property went as
peculium to their owner.[33] Thus, Gaius, in G.3.56, after explaining
the status of Junian Latins, as we have already seen, continues:

> The author of the *lex Junia,* aware that, as a result of that fiction, the
> property of dead Latins would no longer belong to their patrons, since,
> of course, they had not died as slaves so that their goods would have
> belonged as *peculium* to their patrons, nor, as freedmen, would it belong
> by right of manumission to their patrons, thought it necessary, lest the
> benefit conferred on them be turned into a wrong against their patrons,
> to provide that their estates would belong to their patrons just as if the
> statute had not been passed. Hence by that statute the estate of Latins
> goes, as if it were by right of *peculium,* to their manumitters.

Thus, the children of the freedman Latin are excluded from succession. Gaius, in G.3.57–71, discusses further differences between the descent of a freedman's property when he is a citizen and
when he is a Latin, but for us it is enough to notice that as a result of
the *lex Junia* the freedman's inheritance would go to the heirs of the
patron, whereas in the case of a citizen freedman, the patron's rights
descended to his sons and remoter descendents through sons,[34]
though this underwent change as a result of a senatus consultum of
A.D. 42.[35]

Such were the legal bonds between the freedman and his patron. It should, of course, by no means be forgotten that the legal rights and duties were but a small part of the relationship. Socially as well as legally the freedman was usually much inferior, and he frequently remained in a position of intimate dependence on his former master. Often, it seems, the freedman continued to live in the former master's home or in close proximity and perform many of the duties he was used to performing as a slave. Still, there are examples of a master regarding a freedman as a friend and even as a confidant, and this is likely to have been not uncommon. After all, except where a third party provided money for the manumission of a slave or the manumission was imposed on an heir by a legacy or trust, the manumission was almost always a voluntary act of the owner, signifying his respect or affection for the slave and his desire to reward him. Even when the slave had funds in his peculium equal to or greater than his value, the mater was under no compulsion to free him. The peculium, in fact, belonged to the master, and he was at least legally entitled to resume control of it at any time, provided he did not act to defraud creditors. (Still, I have to state that I have never come across any instance in the sources of a master taking over a slave's peculium in the absence of good cause or where an action was pending in respect of it.)

Similarly, when we turn from relations between the freedman and his patron to relations between the freedman and Roman society generally, we see that some of the freedman's disadvantages were not enshrined in law, but, rather, resulted from his low social status, which was exacerbated by his frequent relative poverty. Since many of the relevant texts are not from legal writings and since, moreover, others concern particular historical events, it is not always easy to distinguish between legal and purely social disadvantages. Our concern, of course, is with the law, but that emphasis is not to suggest that social disabilities are not at least as painful. The freedman's legal disabilities vis-à-vis society at large may be divided into two groups: those relating to public law and those relating to private law.

The early Romans were divided into tribes, probably on a residence basis, and the attribution to a tribe was important for

43

voting purposes for much of the Republic. Freedmen were all included in the urban tribes, which in effect restricted the value of their votes. But it is worth noting that the revolting Italian allies who had fought for and eventually obtained citizenship in 90 and 89 B.C. were all included in the same tribes. Freedmen could not be elected to the senate, nor could they be in the highest class of knights, the *equites equo publico* (and usually they did not serve in the infantry, either), and under Gracchan law they could not be judges. Other legal disabilities also existed and varied from time to time, and in 169 B.C., Ti. Sempronius Gracchus wished to disenfranchise freedmen altogether. Despite some doubt, the better view seems to be that none of the legal disabilities affected the children of freedmen.[36] In the Empire, too, certain public and military offices were closed to the freedman.[37] Only equites could take state contracts; hence freedman were banned from these until, in the second century A.D., they could become equites.[38]

The restrictions in private law are not so marked. Contrary to the general view, it seems that in the Republic there was no ban on intermarriage between freeborn and freed persons, though such a marriage might bring social, even censorian, disgrace on a freeborn person of high social status.[39] The lex Julia et Papia forbade marriage between a freedwoman and a senator and his descendants through the male line.[40]

Freedmen thus suffered *legal* disadvantages of various types. But we must not forget that ex-slaves might be economically successful. Thus Pliny records that in 8 B.C. a freedman executed a will in which he declared that, despite heavy losses in the civil war, he nonetheless left 4,116 slaves, 3,600 pairs of oxen, 257,000 other herd animals, and 60 million sesterces in cash.[41] For comparison, the minimum fortune of a senator was 1 million sesterces. The same author relates that, though Crassus (the first Roman to be notorious for wealth) used to say that nobody was wealthy who could not maintain a legion of soldiers on his income, many liberated slaves were subsequently wealthier than he.[42] And Seneca, writing of a rich man of whom he disapproved, stated that he had the bank account and brains of a freedman.[43] Elsewhere he complained of freedmen's conspicuous consumption in building bathing establishments with vast numbers of statues and purely decorative columns.[44] A freedman's wealth was certainly proverbial,[45] even if exceptional.

Four

The Slave as Thing

T hough a successful slave might have manumission and citizenship as his goal, he always remained for the Roman, firmly and realistically, corporeal property whose value could be measured in monetary terms. This chapter is devoted to one aspect of the slave as property, namely, the treatment of the slave as a thing. Nonetheless, the human qualities of the slave will continually emerge. In this regard one significant change of attitude—which will be examined later in the chapter—deserves mention at the outset. At the time of the Twelve Tables of around 450 B.C., the breaking of a slave's bone gave rise to a fixed penalty that was estimated at 50 percent of such an injury to a free man; the slave is treated as a human, though of inferior status. By the time of the *lex Aquilia,* whose final version is probably to be dated to 287 B.C., though relevant portions are older, the killing of, and injuries to, slaves are classed along with the killing of, and injuries to, herd animals.

Though in law a slave could be treated as a thing, the law also stressed his humanity. Indeed, as will emerge continually in the three chapters succeeding this one, in many regards the legal position of a slave was very similar to that of a son—of whatever age—in paternal power. Certainly a free Roman who was still in the power of the father could contract a civil law marriage (with the appropriate consent), whereas a slave was incapable of marriage, but otherwise at private law their positions were very similar. Thus, neither could own any property of any kind,[1] the fund called peculium given for their use by the father or master operated in law irrespective of whether the holder was slave or free, their contracts benefited and bound the father or master to exactly the same extent in exactly the same way, the master acquired property or property rights through them in the same way, and the master was liable at private law for their wrongdoing in the same way (even to the extent that where he could surrender a slave to the victim to exclude his further liability there, he could equally surrender a son). It goes without saying that in practice sons and slaves would be treated very differently. And sons had full public law rights and could hold the highest offices. Slaves also could not be parties in civil law suits.[2]

The Romans divided property into *res mancipi* and *res nec mancipi* until Justinian abolished the distinction. Slaves were classified as res mancipi:

G.2.14a. There is a further[3] division of things: for they are either *mancipi* or *nec mancipi*. *Mancipi* are, for instance, land on Italian soil, likewise buildings on Italian soil, likewise slaves and those animals that are commonly broken in for draught or burden, such as oxen, horses, mules, asses. Likewise, rustic praedial servitudes, for urban praedial servitudes are *nec mancipi*.

Speaking generally we can say that res mancipi represented the more important class of property in an early agricultural society: the stress is obviously laid on what was useful for farmers.[4] The classification was early ossified, and in historic times no additions were made to the list.

The significant feature of the classification is that, whereas corporeal res nec mancipi required actual physical delivery but no formalities for transfer of ownership, res mancipi could only be transferred by a formal ceremony called *mancipatio* or by an adaptation of a legal process called *cessio in iure*:

G.1.119. Now *mancipatio,* as I said above, is a sort of imaginary sale and it, too, is an institution peculiar to Roman citizens. It is performed as follows: When not less than five Roman citizens above the age of puberty are assembled together, with in addition another of the same status who holds the bronze scales and is called the *libripens* (holder of the scales), the person who takes in *mancipatio* speaks thus while holding the bronze: "I declare this slave is mine in accordance with the law of the Roman citizens, and let him have been bought by me with this bronze and with this bronze scale." Then he strikes the scales with the bronze, and he gives the bronze to the person transferring by *mancipatio,* as if it were in place of the price.

Clearly before the introduction of coined money the ceremony was an actual sale, and the purchase price, a specified weight of bronze, was actually weighed out. The ceremony also required the presence of the property to be transferred.[5]

If res mancipi were delivered with the intention of transferring ownership but without a mancipatio, then civil law ownership did not pass. But as a result of the praetor's Edict, the *actio publiciana* was introduced not later than the first century A.D.[6] The wording of this action, as addressed to the judge, ran:[7]

> If Aulus Agerius (the standard name for a plaintiff) bought a slave in good faith and he was delivered to him, then if the slave who is the subject of this action would have been his according to the law of the Roman citizens if he had possessed him for a year, and this is the subject matter of this action, if restitution is not made to Aulus Agerius, condemn Numerius Negidius (the standard name for a defendant) in so much money as the issue is worth. If it does not so appear, absolve him.

The action was also available with respect to other res mancipi, and the period of the prescription for moveables was one year. Thus, when informal delivery and not mancipatio was made to the buyer following a sale, the judge in any action brought by the buyer was to proceed as if the period of prescription had run, and if this would have given the buyer ownership, the judge was to condemn the defendant in whatever would have been due to the owner.

The slave could be the subject matter of a contract such as sale or hire in a way that is basically no different from the sale or hire and so on of other chattels. One or two special features in sale may be noted.

The contract of sale which could be validly formed simply by the agreement of the parties, without fixed formalities, is very much a

Roman invention and is probably to be dated to the third century B.C. Like most great legal inventions, it was not perfect at the outset, and it suffered for a long time from two major defects, namely, that there was no inherent warranty of title or of the buyer's right to undisturbed possession and no inherent warranty against latent defects. The seller's duties were satisfied if he acted in good faith and if he made actual physical delivery of the object sold and had shown proper care until delivery.[8] The buyer was to be protected in two ways, with regard to latent defects and the right to undisturbed possession.

First, the curule aediles—the aediles were the magistrates who had control over the streets and marketplaces—issued an edict relating to the sale of slaves in the Roman market. The earliest version, probably of the early second century B.C., ran:[9]

> See to it that the label of each slave be so written that it can rightly be understood what are the diseases or defects of each, who is a runaway or given to wandering off, or is liable to noxal surrender.[10]

There is no indication in the edict that it gave the buyer a direct remedy against the seller. But this edict was replaced during the Republic by:

> D.21.1.1.1 (Ulpian, book 1 on the *Edict of the Curule Aediles*). The aediles declare: "Let those who sell slaves inform the purchasers what are the diseases and defects of each, who is a runaway or given to wandering off or who is liable to noxal surrender. And when the slaves are sold, let them declare all these matters openly and correctly. But if a slave is sold contrary to these provisions or contrary to what was said or promised when he was sold, in respect of which a legal duty is alleged,[11] we will grant to the buyer and to all whom the matter concerns an action for the redhibition of the slave (within six months of the time when it first became possible to bring an action on that account). But if the slave is made worse after the sale and delivery by the work of the buyer or his household or his procurator, or if anything is born to or acquired by the slave after the sale, and if anything went with the slave as an accessory in the sale, let him make full restitution. Likewise let the seller recover any accessories that he provided. Likewise let sellers declare at the time of sale if the slave had committed a capital crime or had attempted suicide or had been sent into the arena to fight with wild beasts. For we will give an action on such matters. All the more will we give an action if anyone is said to have sold fraudulently, knowingly contrary to these provisions.

Another clause of the edict dealt with the sale of animals in the market. Thus the seller in the market had to declare particular defects, and he was liable if he failed to make the declaration or if he made a false declaration. Fraud or negligence on the seller's part was not needed. Nonetheless, the seller could avoid liability if he made it clear that he was undertaking no guarantees, and this was done by having the slave who was sold wear the pilleus, the cap of liberty.[12] An alternative action that could be brought within one year on the same facts as for the *actio redhibitoria* was the *actio quanto minoris* for the difference between the price paid and a realistic price; later the time periods were two months for the actio redhibitoria, six months for the actio quanto minoris.[13]

The second means of protection for the buyer was to take express guarantees by *stipulatio* from the seller against eviction and against latent defects. These guarantees were traditional, usually, with regard to defects, had much the same scope as the provisions of the aedilician edict, and were at some stage made inherent in the contract of sale, while the provisions of the aedilician edict were generalized to relate to the sale of things, and to all sales, whether made in the market or elsewhere.

There was, of course, considerable controversy as to what counted as *morbus,* disease, and as *vitium,* defect, and the dividing line between them. A few texts will serve as sufficient illustration.

D.21.1.1.7. But it is to be noted that Sabinus defines disease as an unnatural state of the body, which impairs its usefulness for the purpose for which nature gave us bodily health. He says it may sometimes affect the whole body, sometimes only a part (for a disease of the whole body is, for instance, tuberculosis or fever; that of a part, for instance, blindness, even if the slave is so born). He says there is a great deal of difference between a defect and a disease; for instance, if a person stutters he seems more to have a defect than be diseased. But I think the aediles, in order to remove doubt, said the same thing twice, so that no doubt would remain. 8. And thus, if there is any disease or defect which hinders the use and services of the slave, it will give rise to redhibition provided we remember that a very trivial fault will not cause him to be diseased or defective. Thus, it is not a fault not to have declared a light fever or old malaria which can now be disregarded or a minor wound. Therefore, let us give examples of who are really diseased or defective. 9. In the writings of Vivianus the question is raised. If a slave does not always shout his head off among fanatics and somehow prophesies, is he nonetheless to be considered healthy? And Vivianus says he is none-theless healthy, for we ought not to consider persons unhealthy because of a defect of the mind, because otherwise it would be the case that we could deny that many were healthy by sophisticated reasoning, for instance that he was lightminded, superstitious, irritable, stubborn, or had other similar defects of character. The guarantee is given rather on account of the health of the body than of defects of the mind. Some-times, however, a bodily defect reaches the mind and deranges it such as happens to a lunatic as a result of fever. What then is the position? If a defect of the mind is such that an exception of it should be made by the seller, and the seller had said nothing though he was aware of it, he could be liable to the action in the contract of sale.

D.21.1.4.2 (Ulpian, book 1 on the *Edict of the Curule Aediles*). Likewise Pomponius says he gave a reply that gamblers and wine drinkers are not covered by the edict, just as greedy or deceitful or begging or quarrel-some slaves are not covered. 3. Pomponius also says that although a seller is not bound to provide a very intelligent slave, nonetheless if he sells one so silly or moronic that no use can be made of him then there is a defect. But the law seems to be that the terms *disease* and *defect* apply only to the body. The seller will make good a defect of the mind only if he gave an express promise, and otherwise not. That is why the edict expressly refers to wanderers and runaways, since that is a defect of the mind, not of the body. . . . 4. In short, if there is only a defect of the mind, there can be no redhibition unless it was said to be absent and it was not. But an action can be brought on the contract of sale if knowingly he was silent about a defect of the mind.

D.21.1.6 (Ulpian, book 1 on the *Edict of the Curule Aediles*). Pomponius rightly says this edict relates not only to permanent but also to tem-porary disease. 1. Trebatius says a slave with impetigo is not diseased if he can make equally good use of the limb which has the impetigo. And the opinion of Trebatius seems to me to be correct. 2. It seems to me the more correct view that a male slave who lacks generative power is neither diseased nor defective, just as is the case with a slave who has one testicle but is capable of procreating.

D.21.1.7 (Paul, book 11 on *Sabinus*). But if a person is a eunuch to the extent that such a necessary part of the body is lacking then he is diseased.

D.21.1.9 (Ulpian, book 44 on *Sabinus*). Sabinus says one who is dumb is diseased; and it appears that a dumb person is one who has no voice. But one who speaks with difficulty is not diseased, nor is one who speaks indistinctly. Of course, one who speaks unintelligibly is indeed diseased.

D.21.1.11.3 (Ulpian, book 1 on the *Edict of the Curule Aediles*). Caelius says Trebatius drew a distinction in the case of sterility so that if a woman was sterile by nature she was healthy; if as a defect of the body, she was not.[14]

As for the other defects that had to be declared, it is more appropriate to deal with liability to noxal surrender and exactly who was a runaway later in this volume, but we have an important text for the definition of a wanderer, and wandering off was one of the faults that had to be declared under the edict:

D.21.1.17.14 (Ulpian, book 1 on the *Edict of the Curule Aediles*). Labeo defines a wanderer thus, as a cowardly runaway, and, conversely, a runaway as a great wanderer. But we appropriately define a wanderer thus: a person who indeed does not run away, but who frequently wanders without cause and having spent his time in unprofitable pursuits, returns home late.

Slaves might be sold subject to conditions that could have no real application for other goods. A short *Digest* title, 18.7, is dedicated to the subject. Thus, for example:

D.18.7.1 (Ulpian, book 32 on the *Edict*). If a slave was sold under the condition that he not remain in a particular place, the seller is in the position to remit the condition, even to remain in Rome. Papinianus replies the same in book three. For, he says, the condition is observed for the security of the master, so that he is not exposed to danger.

Such a condition, that a slave be exported, was usually protected by a penalty imposed on the buyer in case of breach.

D.18.7.3 (Paul, book 50 on the *Edict*). If a slave is sold under this condition, that he be manumitted within a certain time, then he becomes free if he is not manumitted, provided the seller persevered in his intention. The wishes of an heir are not to be examined.

D.18.7.4 (Marcellus, book 24 of *Digest*). If a person under twenty sold and delivered to you a slave on the understanding that you would manumit him, the delivery is of no effect, even although he delivered with the intention that you would manumit when he became twenty. It makes little difference that he postponed the grant of liberty, for the law stands firm against his intention, which is treated as insufficiently strong.

This text has to be read in the context of the provision of the lex Aelia Sentia that masters under the age of twenty were not permitted to manumit except vindicta and with adequate reason for the manumission shown before a council. Another condition that could have no application to other things was that a sold slave woman not be prostituted.[15]

A slave might also be treated as a thing in a different way and be the object of a legacy. Little need be said about this subject, since it is very much an ordinary part of the law of succession and reveals nothing important about slavery. Thus if a specific slave is the object of the legacy, the heir is to give him as he is. Should the heir by mistake make a promise of quality, the promise is ineffective.[16] The position is rather different when the legacy is simply of a slave to be chosen by the heir:

> D.30.110 (Africanus, book 8 of *Questions*). If an heir, instructed generally to give a slave whom he selected, knowingly gave a thief and he stole from the legatee, Julian said the action for fraud could be brought. But, since the true position is that the heir is bound in this that he not give a very bad slave, he must provide another slave and leave the former in noxal surrender.

But though the heir must not give a very bad slave, he need not give a very good one, and hence he is not bound to give a warranty of quality, though he must guarantee that the slave is not subject to noxal surrender.[17] (This handing over of a wrongdoing slave will be discussed in the next chapter.) The slave who was the object of a legacy could belong to the testator, the heir, or an outsider. If he belonged to the heir and after the testator's death the heir freed him or transferred him to someone who freed him, then the heir had to pay the legatee the value of the slave, even if he had been unaware of the legacy.[18] But when the impossibility of performance of a legacy could not be ascribed to the heir, he was freed from the obligation of performance, and so this was the case where the owner of the slave was an outsider and he had freed the slave. Other aspects of the legacy of a slave may here be ignored.

More significantly, a slave was treated as a thing in that an injury might be done with respect to him, and any right of action would accrue to the master, not to the slave. Slaves had no right to sue. The three principal wrongs in respect of a slave may be said to involve his killing or physical injury, his theft, and assault, physical or verbal, on him. We will treat these in order.

The Twelve Tables of around the mid-fifth century B.C. contained three provisions on physical injury, which may be translated only with difficulty. Thus:

> *Twelve Tables*, 8.2. If a person has burst a part of another person's body (*si membrum rupsit*), let there be retaliation in kind unless he makes agreement for composition with him.[19] 8.3. If with hand or club he has broken a freeman's bone (*si os fregit*), let him undergo a penalty of 300 pieces; if a slave's, 150.[20] 8.4. If he has done simple harm to another, let the penalty be 25 pieces.[21]

How these three provisions relate to one another and together cover the field of physical injury (assuming that they did), and in particular the nature of the distinction between "bursting a part of the body" and "breaking a bone," has long been a matter of dispute. Suggestions include the idea that *Twelve Tables*, 8.2, refers to the use of a cutting instrument, or that that provision relates to the total destruction of a limb. My view is that *Twelve Tables*, 8.2, is a general clause for assaults that involve a deterioration of the body, and hence would include the breaking of a bone, and that the function of 8.3 is simply to set out the minimum penalty when a bone is broken. *Twelve Tables*, 8.4, then, refers to physical assaults where no deterioration occurs.[22] The precise scope of each provision is of less importance for us than the fact that *Twelve Tables*, 8.3, the sole one expressly to mention slaves, clearly treats the slave as a human being, though one of lesser stature than a free person. This was all to be changed by the lex Aquilia, of which the final redaction is traditionally dated by modern jurists to 287 B.C.,[23] though chapter 1[24] is almost certainly earlier:

> D.9.2.2.pr. (Gaius, book 7 on the *Provincial Edict*). The *lex Aquilia* provides in its first chapter: "Whoever wrongfully killed another's male or female slave or four-footed herd animal, let him be condemned to pay to the owner whatever was the highest value in the past year."

In this chapter and again in chapter 3, slaves are classed with domestic animals:

> D.9.2.13.pr. (Ulpian, book 18 on the *Edict*). A free man has on his own account a praetorian action modeled on the *lex Aquilia*. He has not the direct action since no one is regarded as the owner of his own limbs.

A few texts illustrative of the working of chapter 1 of the lex Aquilia are also relevant for our understanding of the position of slaves.

> D.9.2.22.1 (Paul, book 22 on the *Edict*). Likewise, elements of value attaching to the body are taken into account if one kills one of a team of actors or singers or of twins or of a chariot team or of a pair of mules: a valuation must be made not only of the body that was destroyed, but account must also be taken of the amount by which other bodies are depreciated.

Thus, the killing of one of a team of slaves is put on exactly the same level as the killing of one of a pair of mules.

> D.9.2.23.pr. (Ulpian, book 18 on the *Edict*). Hence Neratius writes that if a slave who is instituted heir is killed, the value of the inheritance is also counted. 3. Julian likewise writes that the valuation of the slave killed is made at the time when he was worth most in the past year. Hence if the thumb of a valuable painter was cut off and within a year of the injury he was killed, the owner can bring the Aquilian action and the slave will be valued at the value he had before he lost his skill along with his thumb. 4. But even if a slave was killed who had committed serious frauds in my accounts, and whom I had destined for torture to extract from him the names of his associates, Labeo correctly writes that he is to be valued at the amount of my interest in discovering the slave's frauds, that is, of those committed through him, not at the value of the harm done by him.

> D.9.2.33.pr. (Paul, book 2 on *Plautius*). If you killed my slave, I do not think that personal feelings should be estimated in financial terms; for instance, if someone killed your natural son whom you would have bought at a high price, but only for what he was worth to everybody. Sextus Pedius indeed writes that the prices of things are to be taken generally and not from the feelings of, or usefulness for, individuals. Thus, a person who possesses his natural son is not richer because he would have bought him for a higher figure if someone else possessed him, nor does one who possesses another's son have as much as he could sell him for to the father. For in the *lex Aquilia* we recover the financial

loss; and we are said to have lost either what we could have gained or were forced to pay out.

The basic decision, that damages should be in terms of what the object would generally be reckoned to be worth and not what one individual might pay, is reasonable. Yet the argument of Paul at the end of the text is unconvincing.

> D.9.2.11.pr. (Ulpian, book 18 on the *Edict*). Again, Mela writes: If, when persons were playing with a ball, one of them hit the ball too hard and knocked it against the hands of a barber, and thus the throat of a slave whom the barber was shaving was cut by the razor being jerked against it; in such a case whoever of them is negligent is liable under the *lex Aquilia*. Proculus says the negligence is the barber's; and certainly he is at fault if he was shaving where people habitually played or where the traffic was heavy: nonetheless it is reasonably said that if a person entrusted himself to a barber who had his chair in a dangerous place, he has himself to blame.

> D.9.2.7.4 (Ulpian, book 18 on the *Edict*). If one kills another in wrestling or in the *pancratium* or in boxing, if one kills the other in a public contest, the Aquilian action does not lie, because the damage is thought to have been in the cause of glory and valor, not in the cause of wrongdoing. But this does not apply in the case of a slave, because it is customary only for freeborn persons to enter the contest. But it does apply if a son is injured. Of course if one wounds someone who is giving in, the Aquilian action will lie, or if he kills a slave who is not a party to the contest except where it happens when the master put the slave up to fight: For then the Aquilian action does not lie.[25]

Pancratium was a form of boxing and wrestling combined with kicking and strangling. Biting and gouging were prohibited, but not much else, and it was a highly dangerous sport.

Chapter two concerned a type of fraudulent behavior in contract, but chapter three is again relevant.

> D.9.2.27.5 (Ulpian, book 18 on the *Edict*). The *lex Aquilia* says in the third chapter: "In respect of other things, apart from slaves and herd animals killed, if anyone causes another financial loss because he burnt, broke, or burst (*quod usserit, fregerit, ruperit*) wrongfully, let him be condemned to pay as much to the owner as the matter will appear to be in the next thirty days.

How far this text gives the original wording is disputed, as is the original scope of the chapter. But the best opinion is probably that originally the main purpose was to give an action for the wounding of slaves and four-footed herd animals.[26] The recurrence here of the verbs *rumpere* and *frangere,* found in the Twelve Tables' provisions, would seem to indicate that the chapter was to replace them. Certainly for all periods where we have direct information, the chapter covered injuries to slaves and animals of all types (as well as inaminate things). No text on the lex Aquilia turns on the meaning of frangere, and rumpere has a general significance of causing injury.

> D.9.2.27.17. We accept that the term *rumpere* applies to one who injures with a rod or with a fist or a weapon or anything else so as to cut the slave's body or raise a bruise, but only provided financial loss is wrongfully caused. But if he did not make the slave worse or reduce his price, the Aquilian action will not lie and one will have recourse only to the *actio iniuriarum*. For the Aquilian action pursues only such cases of *rumpere* as cause financial loss. Therefore, even if the value of the slave is not reduced but expenses are incurred in his health and cure, it seems to me that loss is caused and therefore one can sue by the *lex Aquilia*. 28. And if someone castrates a slave boy and makes him more valuable, Vivianus says the Aquilian action does not lie, but an *actio iniuriarum* is to be brought, or one under the aedilician edict or for fourfold.

Not every killing or wounding of a slave gave rise to an Aquilian action, only those done "wrongfully." The relevant term, *iniuria,* was originally taken to mean "without right," but it came to be understood usually as "negligently or maliciously." But, especially when the victim was a slave, the old understanding often retained its force.

> D.9.2.30 (Paul, book 22 on the *Edict*). A person who kills another's slave caught in adultery is not liable under this statute.

> D.9.2.4 (Gaius, book 7 on the *Provincial Edict*). And so if I kill your slave lying in wait to rob me, I shall be safe; for against danger natural reason permits a person to defend himself. 1. The law of the Twelve Tables permits one to kill a thief caught at night, provided he give notice with a shout; a person caught by day, the law allows to be killed if he defends himself with a weapon; in this case, too, notice must be given with a shout.

By the time of Ulpian (and perhaps earlier) it came to be accepted that if in circumstances like those described by Gaius a person preferred to kill than make an arrest he would be liable civilly under the lex Aquilia and criminally for murder of the slave by the lex Cornelia.[27] Paragraph 1 of Gaius seems in the *Digest* to be a historical reminiscence.

Theft was treated primarily as a civil wrong, and a private law action was available to the victim. Slaves, like other property, could be stolen, but two factual peculiarities arise from the human nature of slaves: first, the slave might wish to be stolen, and even assist in his theft; second, the wrongdoer's motive need not simply be financial gain. The two issues are intertwined. There is some conflict in the texts on both issues, and it is tempting to think that the law was not entirely settled or stable.

> D.47.2.36 (Ulpian, book 41 on *Sabinus*). A person who persuaded a slave to run away is not a thief; for a person who gives bad advice does not commit theft, no more than if he persuaded the slave to hurl himself from a height or do himself violence: for these grounds do not give rise to an action for theft. But if one person persuaded him to flee in order that he be seized by another, the former will be liable on the action for theft as if the theft had been committed by his aid and advice. Pomponius further writes that a persuader, even although he is not liable for theft in the meantime, then begins to be liable for theft when anyone becomes the thief of the runaway, the theft being regarded as if it had been by his aid and advice.

The view of Pomponius is, as the wording of the text indicates, more extreme than the opinion expressed in the preceding part of the text, and this can only be the case if he actually held, as he seems to have, that if one person does nothing more than persuade the slave to run away, and the slave does so, and then at some later stage a complete outsider steals the slave, then by a sort of fictional notion the person who persuaded the slave to run away is treated as a thief by complicity. This view, which might be generalized as a claim that, if by one person's deliberate wrongdoing, a factual situation is created which enables another person to steal, then the first person is regarded as an accomplice, seems to appear in other texts but was by no means universally held by the jurists.[28]

An even greater conflict of opinion emerges when we bring D.47.2.61 (Africanus, book 7 of *Questions*) into consideration:

> Just as a runaway female slave is understood to commit theft of herself, so she makes her offspring stolen property by handling it.

Theft is committed by wrongful handling—not necessarily taking away—and the interest of the situation for Africanus is that stolen property cannot be usucapted even in good faith until the property has been returned to the owner. For us it is more interesting to note that if it had been established law that a runaway slave was a thief of himself, then Ulpian, in the text we previously looked at, would have to have held that a person who persuaded the slave to run away was always liable to the action on theft.

Probably in the context of a willing slave victim should be placed D.47.2.68.4 (Celsus, book 12 of *Digest*):

> It is settled that, when a stolen slave steals from the thief, the thief will have on that account an action against the owner so that wrongful deeds of such slaves not only do not go unpunished but also are not a source of profit to their owners.

Buckland observes that this is "a grotesque case, but correct in principle."[29] The reasoning is that a person who had an honest interest in a thing not being stolen was entitled to bring the action on theft, and he did not lose his entitlement simply because he was otherwise dishonest. Thus, in this text the original thief did have an honest interest in the safety of his property, so he could sue the slave's owner for the theft. By the same principle, if an owner steals an object he had given in pledge and it is then stolen from him, he does have an action on theft by virtue of his title as owner.[30] Of course, in our text the slave must have reverted to the control of his master, because actions on account of wrongdoing by a slave lie against the person who has control over him at the time the suit is brought. The master in his turn also had right to sue the thief by the action in theft for the stealing of his slave. Still, the decision seems "grotesque" because the slave was enabled to steal as a result of the plaintiff's own theftuous activity, and the defendant master was entirely innocent and was not in control of the slave at the time of theft. Yet it is entirely in accord with principle.

On the second peculiarity arising from theft because of the human nature of slaves there are four main texts:

> D.4.3.7.7 (Ulpian, book 11 on the *Edict*). Likewise Labeo asks, If you released a slave of mine in chains in order that he flee, should an action in fraud be given? And Quintus, in a note on him, says: "If you did this when you were not guided by pity you are liable to an action for theft; if you were guided by pity, a praetorian action should be given on the facts."

The action on fraud was available only where no other established action was available; hence the very fact that Labeo poses the question in the way he does shows that he excludes the possibility that the action on theft was available. This presumably means he considered that a runaway slave did not steal himself, and hence the person who released him could not be an accomplice in theft. For Quintus the legal position was different. If the motivation for the release was pity, then no action on fraud would be given but simply a remedy on the facts. Otherwise Quintus would allow an action on theft. His opinion is not entirely clear. He could either have considered that the runaway stole himself and therefore the releaser was an accomplice or have held that an intention to make a gain was not needed for theft and that any deliberate conduct inspired by unworthy motives which deprived someone of his property was theft.

The other three puzzling texts should be looked at together:

> D.47.2.83.2 (Paul, book 2 of *Opinions*). A person who, because of lust, carried off a slave woman who was not a prostitute is liable to the action on theft; and; if he keeps her hidden, he is liable to the penalty of the *lex Fabia*.

> P.S.2.31.12. A person who, because of lust, carried off and concealed a prostitute is also, it is settled, liable to the action on theft.

> D.47.2.39 (Ulpian, book 41 on *Sabinus*). It is good law that if a person seized or hid another person's female slave who was a prostitute there is no theft. For we look to the cause of the act, not the act itself; and the cause of the act here was lust, not theft. And therefore, likewise, a person is not liable to the action for theft who, to gratify his lust, broke down the doors of a prostitute's house, and thieves entered who were not led in by him but were acting independently. But would a person who concealed

a whore to gratify his lust be liable under the *lex Fabia?* I do not think he would, and I gave that opinion on an actual case. His behavior is worse than that of a man who steals, but he can set against his disgrace that he is certainly not a thief.

These three texts concern an aspect of the more general problem of whether an intention to make a gain was essential to theft. It should be said that many texts imply that there was such a requirement, but if so, then these others suggest that the requirement could at times be loosely interpreted.[31]

Of the three texts, two survive in Justinian's *Digest,* and they do not actually conflict, though it is difficult to understand why it was theft to carry off a nonprostitute slave to gratify one's lust but not theft to carry off a prostitute slave for the same reason. Nonetheless, that would seem to have been the law in the sixth century. Two texts appear to come from the same book of Paul's *Opinions* and, again, they do not actually conflict, though often doubt has been expressed whether both could have been written by the same author in the same work. There is, of course, total conflict between Paul in *P.S.*2.31.12 and Ulpian in *D.*47.2.39, a conflict made worse by Paul's claim that the law is settled and Ulpian's statement that the contrary is good law. Perhaps one text, more likely that of Paul, does not give the thought of the classical jurist. Or Ulpian was deciding against the common opinion: that may be why his discussion is fuller than is usual. The *lex Fabia,* which is mentioned in two of the texts, was the law that was concerned with kidnapping.

The third major type of wrong where a slave might be the object of the wrong was iniuria, which covered defamation or physical assault of a kind (where slaves were concerned) that did not reduce the slave's value or cause the owner financial expenditure. The praetors issued a number of edicts on iniuria, of which one was expressly concerned with iniuria to slaves:

> *D.*47.10.15.34 (Ulpian, book 77 on the *Edict*). The praetor says: "Whoever is said to have beaten another's slave contrary to good morals or to have put him to examination by torture without authorization of the master, against him I will grant an action. Likewise if anything else is said to have been done [*something here seems to be missing from the text*] I will grant an action after investigation of the facts."

Thus, the edict is really in two parts: where the allegation is that the slave was beaten contrary to good morals or was put to torture without the master's authorization, the praetor will give the action without further ado; where the allegation is of something else, the praetor will grant the action only after consideration of the facts.[32] The text of Ulpian proceeds to elaborate the first part of the edict:

> 38. The edict adds "contrary to good morals" to show that it is not everyone who beats who is liable but one who beats contrary to good morals. If anyone does beat a slave but with the intention of correcting or reforming him, he is not liable. 39. Hence Labeo asks, if a municipal magistrate whips my slave, can I bring the action against him on the charge that he beat him contrary to good morals? And he replies that the judge should investigate what my slave was doing that caused the beating; for the magistrate should not be liable if he struck a slave who impudently sneered at his dignity or badge of office. 40. "To have beaten" is not properly used of someone who struck with his fists. 41. By "examination by torture" we understand torment and bodily pain applied to extract the truth. Therefore mere interrogation or moderate use of terror does not come under this edict. What are called "the bad quarters" are included in the terms "examination by torture." Therefore when any examination is conducted with violence and torment, then "examination by torture is understood."

The actio iniuriarum, of course, could only be brought by the owner, and any award would go to him, but the action might be brought *suo nomine,* on his own account—that is, the master's—or *servi nomine,* on the slave's account. On the former hypothesis the insult was regarded as being to the master, in the latter it was enough that the injury was to the slave. Thus, actions servi nomine would be restricted to the more serious cases, and any action brought under the first part of the edict could be servi nomine. Of course, even when the action was brought on the slave's account the plaintiff would be the owner, since slaves had no legal standing.

> D.47.10.15.35. If anyone does an injury to a slave which is also an injury to the master I believe the master can bring the *actio iniuriarum* on his own account. But even if he did not act with the intention of insulting the master, injury inflicted on the slave should not go unpunished by the praetor, especially if it were done by beating or by examination under torture; for it is clear that the slave also would feel this.

Cases of the action's being brought suo nomine would be when the wrongdoer's behavior constituted an invasion of the master's proprietary rights, as in *D.9.2.27.28*, where a slave boy was castrated without authority, or when the wrongdoer's intention was to insult the master through the vehicle of the slave. Thus:

> *D.47.10.15.45.* Sometimes the injury done to a slave rebounds to the master, sometimes not. For Mela writes that I cannot sue a person for injury to me if he would not have struck a slave had he known he was mine; a slave, that is, who was behaving like a free man or whom he thought was another's rather than mine.[33]

When the action was servi nomine under the second part of the edict, the injury must not have been too slight:

> *D.47.10.15.44.* Thus the praetor does not promise an *actio iniuriarum* on account of the slave in all instances. For if he was only lightly struck or not grossly abused verbally he will not give an action. But if the slave was defamed by an act or by scurrilous verses I think the praetor's investigation of the facts should be extended to the quality of the slave: for it makes a great deal of difference what kind of slave he is, whether he was a frugal, methodical household steward or in fact very ordinary or a drudge or some such. And what if he was chained, or known to be of bad character, or even branded? Thus the praetor will take account both of the nature of the alleged injury and of the person of the slave alleged to be injured, and so he will permit or refuse the action.

There were, of course, other minor instances in which a master had an action for an injury to him when a slave was the object. The most important is probably the edict for making a slave worse:

> *D.11.3.1.pr.* (Ulpian, book 23 on the *Edict*). The Praetor says: "Whoever is said to have with deliberate wrongful intention taken in another's male or female slave or persuaded him or her to do something which made him or her worse, against him I will give an action for double the matter in issue."

The edict then apparently went on to state that a noxal action would be given when the wrongdoer was a male or female slave.[34] The action lay whether the slave was made physically or morally worse, and damages were not restricted to a diminution in the value of the slave:

> D.11.3.16 (Alfenus Varus, book 2 of *Digest*). A master freed a slave who
> was his household superintendant and then received the accounts from
> him. When the accounts were not in order he discovered that the slave
> had spent the money with a certain little woman. The question was
> raised whether he could bring the action for making a slave worse
> against that woman, since the slave was now free. I replied that he could,
> but he could also sue on theft for the money that the slave had brought
> her.

I have reserved for the end of the chapter a topic of consuming
social and legal interest which might have been dealt with under
theft but wherein the slave, although the object, can scarcely be
thought a victim. I refer to the law of the sale of runaway slaves.[35]
What was in issue was, from the point of view of the masters and the
authorities, a wicked racket. A slave who wished to get himself
owned by a particular new master or, more likely, wanted to obtain
his freedom would run away, taking with him his peculium or
property belonging directly to his master. He would then contact a
slave catcher (slave catching was a profession that existed from
quite early in the Republic), and a deal would be worked out. The
slave catcher would approach the master, persuade him to sell to
him the runaway at a fraction of his value, as a speculation. The
slave catcher would then "find" the runaway and, in consideration
of property given him by the slave, would either transfer the slave to
another owner or manumit him. (Manumission, as we saw in
chapter 2, would give the slave full citizenship if it occurred one
year after he was possessed by the slave catcher.) How was the law
to cope with this and similar situations?

A first step that might have been of some service was the lex Fabia
of the late Republic[36] which, among other provisions, prohibited
the buying and selling of another's slave without the owner's
knowledge and established the high penalty of fifty thousand
sesterces. This penalty against both buyer and seller was then
extended by a senatus consultum to any buying or selling of a
runaway slave who had not been recaptured.[37] Consequently, an
owner who accepted the slave catcher's offer could find himself in
serious trouble; and, at that, all the more easily since the action was
popularis, that is, it could be brought by anyone. The sale, more-

over, would be void.[38] The senatus consultum contained a reasonable minor exception, and the exception, together with one response of the slave catchers to the senatus consultum, is revealed by
a rescript of the emperors Diocletian and Maximian of the year A.D.
287 addressed to a woman called Marciana:

> C.9.20.6. It is settled that it is not permitted to sell or make a gift of a
> slave in flight. From this you will understand you are in breach of the
> law which laid down for such wrongs a certain penalty to be paid to the
> imperial treasury; except that it is permitted to coheirs and partners in
> dividing the common property to make an auction among themselves. It
> is permitted to sell a runaway, on the terms that only then is the sale
> effective, when he had been recovered and demanded by the buyer.

Thus, the senatus consultum refused the action with a penalty
when the sale of the runaway slave was made by coheirs and
partners wishing to divide the property, provided the sale was to
the highest bidder among coheirs or partners themselves. One
response to the senatus consultum, it seems, was to make a gift of
the runaway slave, and it seems a fair hypothesis that the gift would
be met with a disguised return from the slave catcher. Daube rightly
points out that the gift, to be complete, would have to be by
mancipatio, and only around the third century could absent property validly be mancipated; hence, to judge from C.9.20.6, legis-
lators had caught up with the device fairly quickly.[39] Even earlier,
another device had been adopted which seems to have had innocent beginnings:

> D.18.1.35.3 (Gaius, book 18 on the *Provincial Edict*). If someone gave a
> mandate to a friend going abroad to look for his runaway slave and, if he
> found him, to sell him, he does not offend against the senatus consultum
> because he did not sell, nor does his friend because he sold a slave who
> was present. Moreover, the buyer who bought the slave who was not
> absent is understood to have acted properly.

When this decision became a general rule[40] it was open to abuse,
and the friend would be replaced by rogue slave catchers. A variant
dodge is also described as valid by Ulpian:

> D.48.15.2.2 (book 9 on the *Duties of the Proconsul*). It must further be
> said that, if someone gave a mandate to Titius to catch his runaway slave

on the condition that if he caught him he had bought him, the *senatus consultum* does not apply.

Thus, the slave catcher is given a mandate to find, plus a conditional sale to him if the slave is caught; for all practical purposes the senatus consultum was circumvented.

Final victory on this issue between slave catchers and the law was achieved by the law by a rule attacking the problem from a different angle:

> P.S.1.6a.1. A slave bought by a slave catcher cannot be manumitted within ten years without the consent of his former owner.[41]

Slaves might still run away and still steal from their owners, but they could have no hope of acquiring freedom and citizenship through the intervention of a slave catcher.

Five

The Slave as Man: Noncommercial Relations

As we have seen, a slave might be the object of a wrong regarded legally as done to his master, but the slave might also be the wrongdoer. The scope for mischief was wide, since slaves could be found in many walks of life, and very many slaves were not confined to working the large estates. The law is particularly interesting with regard to the master's liability. No action at private law could be brought against a slave, because a slave had no legal standing. Much use was made at Rome of private actions—though criminal prosecutions were also possible—where we would instinctively think only of criminal sanctions. This is true not only for theft, but also even for the deliberate wounding or killing of slaves, who were regarded as property.

The basic rule when a slave committed a civil wrong and an action was brought against the person who had control of the slave when the action was brought, was that the defendant had the choice either of paying the amount of condemnation, which was the same as if a free person had committed the delict, or of surrendering the slave to the plaintiff. In effect this was an early system of limited liability.

D.9.4.1 (Gaius, book 2 on the *Provincial Edict*). Those actions are called noxal actions which arise not from contract but which are brought against us on account of the harm (*noxa*) or wrongdoing of slaves. The force of these actions is that if we are condemned, we are permitted to avoid the amount of the suit by the surrender of the wrongdoer's person.

The rules varied slightly from one delict to another, and a system was already in operation by the mid-fifth century B.C. under a provision of the Twelve Tables. The basic text is *D*.9.4.2 (Ulpian, book 18 on the *Edict*):

If a slave kills with the knowledge of his master he makes the master liable for the total sum because the owner himself is regarded as having killed. But if he killed without the master's knowledge the action is noxal because the master ought not to be liable for a slave's wicked deed in more than that he surrender him for the harm. 1. He who does not prohibit, whether he remains or ceases to be the owner, is liable to this action; for it is enough that he was master at that time when he did not prohibit, to the extent, as Celsus thinks, that if the slave is alienated in whole or in part or is manumitted the injury does not follow the person (*noxam caput non sequi*): for a slave did nothing wrong who obeyed his master's orders. And certainly if the master ordered the slave this can be said: but if he simply did not prohibit, how will we excuse the slave's deed? But Celsus draws a distinction between the *lex Aquilia* and the law of the Twelve Tables. For under the old statute, if a slave without the knowledge of his master committed theft or another wrong, the action is noxal on account of the slave, and the master is not liable on his own account; but under the lex Aquilia, he says, the owner is liable on his own account, not on account of the slave. He gives the explanation of both laws; of the Twelve Tables that it wished slaves in the matter not to obey their masters; of the *lex Aquilia* that it excused a slave who obeyed the master because the slave would be killed if he did not obey. But if the view of Julian expressed in his eighty-sixth book is approved that "If a slave committed theft or inflicted harm" also applies to later laws, then it may be said that also on account of the slave one may proceed against the owner in the noxal action so that the fact that the Aquilian action is given against the owner does not excuse the slave but does burden the owner. We approved the opinion, which is both reasonable and approved by Marcellus commenting on Julian.

This text of Ulpian is very instructive regarding Roman legislation, the argumentation of the jurists, and expressed attitudes toward slaves, as well as for the substantive law. Thus the Twelve Tables contained an express provision on noxal surrender of which the text gives part of the (modernized) wording. The provision spoke of the commission of theft and of other harm. If the provision was not regarded as applying wholly to the lex Aquilia, then the lex Aquilia would also seem to have contained words on noxal surrender, a view borne out by G.4.76:

> Noxal actions are established either by law or by the praetorian Edict: by laws, for instance, for theft, by the law of the Twelve Tables [and] for wrongful damage to property, by the *lex Aquilia;* by the praetorian Edict, for instance, for *iniuria* and for robbery with violence.

Apart from what seems to be the obvious implication of the passage, the edicts relating to iniuria and robbery with violence were two of the very few which we know contained express provisions on noxal surrender. Nevertheless, the view of Julian, in D.9.4.2.1, that the Twelve Tables' provision applies to the Aquilian matter under discussion indicates that the clause of the lex Aquilia did not expressly regulate the actions where the master was aware of the slave's wrongdoing.

To come now to the substance in D.9.4.2. For the discussion of killing, what is at issue is not a criminal action but the private law action under the lex Aquilia. For a long time, including the whole of the Republic, it was not murder deliberately to kill another's slave. Fr. 1 at the beginning makes it clear that the person who is liable to the noxal action is the owner or other person who has control at the time the action is brought. This is the meaning of the standard phrase "*caput noxa sequitur*" ("The injury follows the person"), whose negative form appears in the text. The rule is almost inevitable once one accepts that noxal surrender is a form of limited liability, but it can cause problems, especially when the slave has committed delicts on a number of citizens. In such a case, if the owner surrendered the slave to the first plaintiff, it would be that plaintiff who would be the defendant in a subsequent action brought on account of wrong committed even before his own action. The Romans never resolved the legal problems inherent in the situation. When a slave committed a series of wrongs against different people, the victim who sued *last* would retain the slave or receive the full compensation (or penalty). Should the slave die after joinder of issue, the master remained liable—for the whole amount of the condemnation, under Justinian, though in classical law he could escape further liability if he surrendered the dead body.[1]

The main issue in the present text, though, is liability when the master either had commanded the delict or had known of the slave's intention and did not forbid him from carrying it out. There seems to have been a difference here between theft and damage to property. The wording of the text may seem strange, but mainly this is because its original context was a discussion of the lex Aquilia, and it is that statute that is under discussion unless we are expressly told otherwise. Where the master had known of or ordered the intended wrong, the jurist Celsus held that for theft the action was noxal and the master was not liable on his own account, but that for damage to property the owner was liable on his own account. The corollary, as Celsus's reasoning indicates, is that if the slave becomes free, he is liable personally to an action on the theft committed while he was a slave, but not to an action under the lex Aquilia. Julian, Marcellus, and Ulpian all seem to have accepted that an action lay against the master on his own account under the lex Aquilia, but they claimed that the Twelve Tables' provision also applied to the lex Aquilia; hence the slave (become free) was also liable to an action under the lex Aquilia. Ulpian's rhetorical question seems to indicate, though, that for the lex Aquilia the freed slave will not face the action if he was obeying his master.

Celsus's argumentation is not convincing. To begin with, the suggestion that the slave had reason to fear being killed if he did not obey the master's command to offend against the lex Aquilia but not if he refused to steal fails to take account of the fact that the lex Aquilia gave an action not only for killing but also for minor physical assaults. Again, Celsus's reasoning is postulated on the master's ordering the wrong, but the rules apply equally where the master simply failed to prohibit. An easier solution might be to suggest a difference in the understanding of causation or simply in interpretation. Thus, the Twelve Tables' words were taken to apply to every case when the slave performed the wrongful act. If he stole, the provision relating to noxal surrender applied, and the owner would have the right of surrender. Whether the owner had commanded the act or knew of the slave's intention was treated as irrelevant. That this approach could have unfortunate results was recognized by the time of the lex Aquilia, hence within its scope the master was held liable on his own account if he ordered the wrongful act or knew of the slave's intention and did not forbid him. The jurists were then left to work out the slave's liability, an issue that would only arise if he had been manumitted or alienated. Where the slave had acted on his own initiative but with the master's knowledge, there was a difference of opinion. Celsus's solution is doctrinally the purer, but that of Julian the more morally reasonable. It is, however, rather clumsy to hold the slave liable under the lex Aquilia but on the basis of an older statute.

Noxal liability could vary slightly from one delict to another in other instances, as well. A striking variant occurs in iniuria, where the noxal action is the subject of a specific praetorian edict whose wording has not survived.[2] But it seems that the edict gave the defendant master another option before final condemnation: if the judge approved, the master could hand over the slave for a beating.[3] Presumably, the judge would allow this only if the original iniuria had been slight.

Particular complexities could arise when the wrongdoer was a statuliber:

> D.9.4.14.1 (Ulpian, book 18 on the *Edict*). But even if he were a *statuliber* and before his surrender the condition of his freedom was fulfilled, or liberty left by trust was granted, or ownership was transferred on the fulfillment of a condition on a legacy, the defendant ought to be released at the option of the judge. It is also part of the judge's duty that a guarantee be given to the person who takes the slave, against eviction arising from the defendant's own act.

> D.9.4.15 (Gaius, book 6 on the *Provincial Edict*). The praetor should decree that a transfer of the action be made against the *statuliber*. If at the time of judgement the freedom is still in suspense, Sabinus and Cassius think the heir is released by delivering the slave, because he is giving up all his right. This view is correct.

These texts demonstrate a reasonable derogation from the general principle that events after the joinder of issue do not affect the defendant's liability. In the absence of any such derogation the action would still lie against the defendant, even though the slave had become free. Thus, the defendant would have no power to surrender the slave and would have to pay the full amount of the condemnation. Since after joinder of issue no other action could be brought on the same facts, no further action could be brought against the delinquent slave, who is now free. Hence the derogation: the judge might release the defendant if the statuliber obtained his freedom, but then it would become necessary, as the text of Gaius shows, for the praetor formally to decree the transfer of the action against the former statuliber if the plaintiff is to have any redress. The kind of legal problem that might arise is illustrated by D.47.2.62.9 (Africanus, book 7 of *Questions*):

> An heir was defending in a noxal action a *statuliber* who was to obtain his freedom if he gave ten gold pieces. Before completion of the case the slave acquired his freedom by giving the ten to the heir. The question is asked whether release ought to be given only if the heir gave the ten gold pieces he received to the plaintiff. Julian held that it depended on the source of the money, so that if it came from any source other than the *peculium* the heir will have to hand it over, since if the slave had not yet achieved his freedom he would have been noxally surrendered and would have given the money to the surrenderee [i.e., to the plaintiff]: but if it came from the *peculium* the opposite must be held, because he gave the heir the heir's own money.

Though the text does not say so, we can presume that a transfer of judgement had been given against the former statuliber. The question that interested the jurists was the fate of the money given by the slave for his freedom. The solution is to put the defendant in the position he would have been in had the suit been settled at the moment of joinder of issue. Thus, since on surrender he would have retained the peculium, he keeps the ten gold pieces if they came from that; and since he would not have received the money from an outside source, he has to hand over the sum if the gold pieces were received otherwise than from the peculium. But the plaintiff's position has dramatically improved in the second alternative. In the absence of formal transfer of action, joinder of issue would have blocked any further right of action, so if the case had run its course, the plaintiff would have no further claim once noxal surrender was made to him. If at that stage someone paid the ten gold coins and the statuliber obtained his freedom, the victim would not have been able to sue the former slave again on the delict. But as a result of the transfer of action, now he can, and he also takes the ten gold pieces from the heir. Presumably, though, the judicial award will take account of the ten that have been paid.

It was a basic principle of the Roman law of delict that joint wrongdoers were each fully liable in the delictal action. Thus, the condemnation in the action for theft was double (or, in some circumstances, four times) the value of the stolen property, and if there were two wrongdoers, each would have to pay this amount. Logically this would have meant that if several slaves belonging to the same person committed a delict, then he would be liable for as many full condemnations as there were wrongdoing slaves, though he could avoid paying by surrendering all of the slaves to the victim. But in such circumstances the praetor limited the liability to what would have been due if one free man had committed the act; alternatively, the owner could surrender all of the slaves. The origins of this approach are to be found in an edict concerning theft,[4] but it was extended to other delicts:

D.9.2.32.pr. (Gaius, book 7 on the *Provincial Edict*). It has been asked whether the proconsul's practice with regard to theft committed by a household of slaves (that is, that the demand for a penalty is not allowed in respect of each one, but it is enough if payment is made such as if one free man had committed the theft) should also be observed in the action for wrongful damage. The better opinion is that the same practice should be observed, and rightly. For the rationale with regard to the action for theft that an owner should not lose his whole household for one delict applies similarly in an action for wrongful damage, hence it follows that the condemnation should similarly be assessed, especially because the basis of this delict may be slighter—for instance, if the loss is caused negligently and not deliberately.

This approach was not adopted, however, for all delicts, since, for example, in iniuria, the act of each slave could be treated as a separate wrong.[5]

A further very special case, and one that has been the subject of much scholarly debate,[6] concerns the liability of a master for a jointly owned slave who has injured the other master.

> D.9.2.27.1 (Ulpian, book 18 on the *Edict*). If a common slave (belong-ing, that is, to you and me) killed my slave, the *lex Aquilia* will apply against you, if he acted with your consent: and Urseius reports that this was Proculus's opinion. But if he acted without your consent, the noxal action does not lie, lest it be in the power of the slave to decide whom he will serve.[7] I think this opinion is correct.

The decision is straightforward where one master authorized the wrong against the other. Where he did not, the text tells us that the noxal action will not lie, and this can only mean that no action at all will be available under the lex Aquilia. This is confirmed by other texts, and particularly by D.47.2.62.pr. (Africanus, book 8 of *Questions*):

> If a common slave stole from one of his owners, it is settled that the owner should sue by the action for division of common property (*actio communi dividundo*), and it is in the choice of the judge to order that the loss be made good or a share in the slave be ceded.[8]

The victim is, thus, not left without a remedy, but can sue by the action for the division of common property, which is a particularly suitable choice, since the judge had very great discretion in making his award. The noxal action was not appropriate because, apart from the theoretical problem of holding that it was your share of our slave that interfered with my property, the condemnation in a delictal action (particularly theft) could involve more than mere compensation, and it was in the circumstances unreasonable to consider the defendant more at fault than the plaintiff. The reason-ing of Ulpian in D.9.2.27.1 (if the text has been correctly recon-structed) is not persuasive, since it would make as much sense in every case of deliberate damage by a slave to another's property, where noxal surrender was permitted.

It could easily happen that a slave's delict was also a breach of a contract made between the victim and the slave's owner or the slave himself. The clear, basic rule when a breach of contract was also a delict was that the victim could choose whether to proceed in an action on contract or on delict. But the intervention of a slave added a complication:

> Coll.12.7.9. But if the slaves of a tenant burned down the tenement, Urseius, in book 10, says that Sabinus gave the answer that the owner

should be sued under the *lex Aquilia* in a noxal action on account of the slaves; but he held that the owner was not liable to an action on the lease. But Proculus replied when slaves of a tenant farmer burned down a country house that the tenant would be liable either on the lease or under the *lex Aquilia,* the tenant being able to give the slaves in noxal surrender. If the matter was settled in one action, the other could not also be brought.

The text reveals a dispute between Sabinus and Proculus. Sabinus held that where the master had made a contract and a slave committed a wrong within the scope of it, the master had not breached the contract and could not be sued under it by the relevant contractual action. But the action on delict could be brought against the master. Proculus allowed the other contracting party a choice of either the contractual or the delicted action. The text also shows Proculus permitting noxal surrender of the slave in the contractual action, but many scholars find this so strange that they believe this part of the text is due to postclassical interpolation. There is not enough textual evidence to reach a secure conclusion.[9]

Sabinus's opinion was unsuccessful and was dropped from the *Digest,* where the same text appears at *D.*9.2.27.11 (Ulpian, book 18 on the *Edict*) with a continuation of the discussion of noxal surrender:

But if he had injurious slaves, then he is liable for wrongful damage because he had that kind of slave.

That is, if the tenant was at fault in having that kind of slave, he loses the right of noxal surrender because he is directly responsible for the injury.[10]

As befits the subject of this book, we have dealt only with the noxal surrender of slaves. But to keep a proper balance it should be mentioned here that sons in power could also be surrendered in classical law. One of the most striking features of Roman law to the modern observer—namely, that wrongs are treated primarily as delicts and not as crimes—results from the prominence of slaves and sons in wrongdoing. In modern times, whatever the state of the law, it is seldom worth the victim's while to sue civilly a thief or someone who assaulted him physically or caused deliberate criminal damage, since so frequently the wrongdoer would be in no position to pay damages. Things were different in Rome. No doubt frequently a free person sui iuris who committed a wrong would also be unable to pay a civil penalty, but where the wrongdoer was a son or a slave, the victim would be sure to receive either the sum of money calculated by law or, alternatively, the surrender of the son, to work off the amount that the condemnation would have been, or the slave, whom he could then either keep or sell.

The law of theft also developed very particular actions that are best explained on the basis that wrongdoers were often sons or slaves:

> G.3.186. There is said be *furtum conceptum* when stolen property is sought for and found on a man's premises in the presence of witnesses. Against him, even though he is not the thief, a particular action is established which is called the *actio furti concepti*. 187. There is said to be *furtum oblatum* when stolen property has been passed on to you by someone, provided it was passed on to you with the intention that it be found on your property rather than on his who was responsible for the passing on. . . . 191. For *conceptum* and *oblatum* the penalty under the Twelve Tables is threefold, and this is retained by the praetor.

In a state where there was no organized police force, it could well make sense to provide that a person on whose premises stolen property was found was to be treated as a thief unless he could establish his freedom from guilt. But the Twelve Tables went further, and the provision was to the effect that that person was liable even if he was not the thief; moreover, the code established a penalty that was more than that for ordinary theft but less than that for manifest theft. It should be mentioned that if stolen property was found after a ritual search, the delict was declared by the Twelve Tables to be manifest theft.[11] The approach of the compilers of the ancient code becomes more understandable if we bear in mind that where the person on whose premises the stolen property was found was not himself the thief, a son or a slave of his usually would be, and the head of the household was always liable in any event for their misbehavior. But consequent upon this approach, for the situation where neither the householder nor one of his dependents was the wrongdoer, the Twelve Tables gave the house-holder an action for the same amount against the person who passed the stolen property on to him. The burden of finding the guilty party was thus transferred to him. The qualification of Gaius that the *actio furti concepti* lay only if the passing on was with the intention that the stolen property be found with that householder rather than with the person who did the passing is very likely not to have existed at the time of the Twelve Tables, but to be the result of later interpretation.[12]

Before we leave wrongdoing by slaves, we should look at one particular case:

> D.47.2.52.15 (Ulpian, book 37 on the *Edict*). A slave who pretended to be a free man in order to obtain a loan of money does not commit theft; for he does nothing more than declare he is a person suitable to be a debtor. The same rule applies to one who pretended to be a *paterfamilias,* when he was a son in power, so that money might be lent to him more readily.

The text does not present a legal difficulty. In general, theft was committed by wrongful handling contrary to the owner's wishes.[13] Here the owner is willing to hand over the money; he has only been deceived as to the status of the recipient. Rather, what the text reveals is the difficulty of distinguishing between a Roman free man and a Roman slave, a difficulty we have already observed elsewhere[14] and which can arise in many contexts. For instance, it is the express reason given by Paul for allowing the sale of a free man as a slave to be a valid contract of sale.[15]

If we leave aside commerce, then it is the field of delict in which we most often come across the slave in the legal sources as an active participant. It is not easy to find legal texts that show slaves as holders of family relationships.[16] The absence of legal regulation is in marked contrast to the funerary inscriptions and literary sources that show that it was very common for slaves to live together in a familial relationship that much resembled marriage. At law, slaves could not be married, not even with one another:

> *Epit. Ulp.* 5.5. With slaves there is no marital capacity.

Thus, if a free person became a slave, for instance through capture by the enemy, the marriage ended.[17] And so also:

C.9.9.23 (Diocletian and Maximian, A.D. 290). Slaves cannot make an accusation of adultery because of a violation of their cohabitation.

Though nature may break through, the law remains firm:

D.38.10.10.5 (Paul, sole book on *Degrees of Relationship*). We do use these names of blood relatives even in the case of slaves. And so we speak of fathers and sons and brothers even of slaves. But these servile blood relationships have nothing to do with the laws.

Therefore, there could be no succession on death to a slave through blood relationships:

C.65.9.4. (Diocletian and Maximian, A.D. 294). A slave cannot have successors on death.[18]

At times, though, the law did take the relationships into account:

D.33.7.12.33 (Ulpian, book 20 on *Sabinus*). The household companions of slaves, that is, wives and children, are contained in a legacy of an estate with its equipment.

The background is the discussion of the extent of a legacy of a "farm with its equipment," and it was settled that slaves who worked the farm were part of the equipment.

Another text gives as the reason for the decision that the testator is not interpreted as having wished such a cruel separation.[19] So what is involved is not a legal rule, but the question of interpretation of an individual's last will and testament, and in different circumstances a different interpretation could be preferable:

D.33.7.20.4 (Scaevola, book 3 of *Replies*). Likewise he raised the question in the case of the legacy of a business manager whether his wife and daughter were included in the legacy, when the manager resided not on an estate but in town. He replied that nothing was said to justify their going with the legacy.[20]

But there were some relevant legal rules:

C.3.38.11 (Constantine, A.D. 334 [?]). Divisions of property should be made in such a way that close relations among slaves or serfs should remain with one single successor. For who will tolerate that children be separated from parents, sisters from brothers, wives from husbands? Therefore if people took slaves or serfs off to different legal families, they are compelled to return them together again.[21]

The rescript is considering the actions for division of property, actions which normally gave the judges great discretion. The appropriate principle also emerges elsewhere:

> D.21.1.35 (Ulpian, book 1 on the *Edict of the Curule Aediles*). Often on account of diseased slaves even healthy slaves are redhibited, if they cannot be separated without great difficulty or without an offense against piety. For what if they wished to retain a son and redhibit the parents? Or vice versa? And this ought to be observed both in the case of brothers and of persons joined in a settled domestic relationship.

This text relates to the sale of slaves where, under the aedilician edict, a diseased slave could be returned to the seller within a certain time. Again, on the termination of a marriage, when the dowry was returned to the wife, the husband retained accessions, but this rule did not apply to children born to slaves who were part of the dowry:

> C.5.13.1.9a (Justinian, A.D. 530). Therefore the offspring of slave women forming part of a dowry—that is, where the dowry was not estimated in money—or whatever dotal slaves acquire on any ground other than through the property of the husband or their own work, belong to the woman whichever of the two actions is used. 9b. But the offspring of draught animals and everything which is contained in the concept of fruits does pertain to the profit of the husband for the time of the marriage, whether they were or were not estimated in money.

Something more is also involved here. Where the accessions to the dowry came through a slave forming part of the dowry, the husband took whatever accession resulted from the slave's work or from the husband's own property, and the wife took all other accessions, such as those resulting from a gift to the slave. This by itself would not necessarily resolve the issue of who should take the children of a dotal slave woman. Other animal offspring, however, would go to the husband as "fruits" or accessions. But the jurists, recognizing their human nature, refused to regard slave children as "fruits."

> D.47.2.48.6 (Ulpian, book 42 on *Sabinus*). Foals born to mares that are stolen property immediately belong to the purchaser in good faith; rightly, because they count as fruit. But the offspring of a slave woman is not counted as fruit.

Thus, likewise, a possessor of something in good faith was entitled to take the fruits, but not the children born to a slave. And a similar rule applied, as we shall see, in usufruct. Blood relationships of slaves were also taken into account in criminal law under the *lex Pompeia* for parricide. The crime was committed by killing a person in a particular degree of relationship, and such relationship was considered to exist even between slaves.[22]

The manumission of slaves not only drastically changed their social status but made much more meaningful—so far as law was concerned—their personal relationships:

> D.23.2.14.2 (Paul, book 35 on the *Edict*). Servile blood relationships must also be observed in this legal context. Therefore, a slave who is manumitted must not marry his mother; the law is the same in the case of a sister and the daughter of a sister. Similarly, it must be said on the other hand that a father may not marry his daughter if they were freed from slavery, even if there is doubt as to whether he was the father. For a natural father must not marry his illegitimate daughter, since in contracting marriage natural law and decency are to be regarded: it is contrary to decency to marry one's daughter. 3. The law established for servile relationships of blood is also to be observed in servile "relationships by marriage"; for instance, I may not marry the woman who was in a stable relationship with my father, as if she were my step-mother; and on the other hand, a father may not marry a woman who was in a stable relationship with his son, as if she were his daughter-in-law. Likewise, we cannot marry the mother of the woman one had as a wife while one was a slave, as if she were a mother-in-law. For since servile relationships by blood can be envisaged, why not also "relationships by marriage"? In a doubtful area it is more certain and more proper to refrain from marriage of this kind.

Apart from marriage, rules of law on such matters seem to have existed in classical law only with regard to the prohibition of bringing an action against particular categories of persons:

> D.2.4.4.3 (Ulpian, book 5 on the *Edict*). Labeo thinks that the term "parents" also includes those who recognized as theirs a child during slavery; and not, as Severus said, only legitimate children. But even if a son is illegitimate, he must not take his mother to court.

Justinian was responsible for an important reform:

J.3.6.10. It is certain that that part of the edict that promises possession of the estate does not apply to servile blood relationships: such relationship was not calculated by any ancient statute. But by the constitution which we issued on the law of patronage (which law until our time was rather obscure, cloudy, and confused in all respects), we, impelled by humanity, also conceded that if a person in a servile union had a child or children, whether the woman was free or a slave, or on the other hand a slave woman had, through a free man or a slave, children of either sex, and the parents obtain their freedom, and those who were born while the mother was a slave also earn their liberty, or where the mothers were free the fathers were slaves and later achieved freedom, then they all succeed to their father or mother, and the rights of patronage are set aside to that extent. By a special provision of that law, we granted such children succession rights not only to their parents but also mutual rights of succession among themselves, whether there are only those born in slavery and later manumitted or also others who were conceived after the liberty of their parents; and whether they are by the same father or the same mother, or by different marriages in the same way as those born in lawful marriage.

Previously, of course, in classical law, problems of interpretation of wills had occurred:

D.28.8.11 (Javolenus, book 4 of the *Posthumous Works of Labeo*). A person who had a freedman son appointed him heir, and then wrote: "If I have no son who reaches full age then let my slave Dama be free." There was no son except the freedman son, who was not of full age. The question was asked whether Dama was free. Trebatius says no, because a freed person is also included in the term *son*. Labeo takes the opposite view because in that situation a lawful son is to be understood. I approve the opinion of Trebatius, provided it appears the testator was speaking of that son.

Naturally a slave could not bring a legal action, nor could he be sued, except in criminal law. The incapacity of slaves in the process—except in a limited way as witnesses—gave rise to some interesting and quite exceptional law. For instance, a praetorian edict sought to give protection against a recent widow's wrongly claiming to give birth to her dead husband's child, and arranged for the appointment of "guardians of the womb." These guardians by the very wording of the edict[23] could not be slaves, presumably because it was likely that the guardians would have to give evidence, and evidence by slaves was not easily to be admitted. Despite the wording of the edict, an exception was made to a certain extent:

> D.25.4.1.13 (Ulpian, book 24 on the *Edict*). But even if a slave was appointed heir provided no child was born, then Aristo writes that to this slave also, although not all, yet nonetheless some, rights should be conceded, at the option of the praetor, with regard to safeguarding the birth. I think this opinion is correct. For it is in the public interest that there be no supposititious child, so that the dignity of rank and the family be safeguarded. And therefore even that slave, since he has been given hope of succession, just as he is, ought to be listened to when he is looking after public interests and his own affairs.

Another praetorian edict provided that if work was being done or was about to be done that might injure a neighbor's land, the neighbor might give notice and then bring the owner before the praetor:

> D.39.1.5.1 (Ulpian, book 52 on the *Edict*). Notice of "new work" may be made to a slave; but he cannot give notice, nor does such notice have any effect.

The explanation is that notice, not being formal, could be given to a slave as his master's representative, but since giving notice was the first step toward a legal process, it could not be given by a slave.

A slave could not act as accuser in a criminal trial. Oddly this might at times be beneficial to a slave:

> D.48.10.24 (Scaevola, book 22 of his *Digest*). A slave, Aithales, to whom, under the will of Betitus Callinicus, freedom and part of the inheritance was left under a *fideicommissum* from people who were appointed heirs in eleven shares, made an accusation to Maximilla, the daughter of the testator and heir to a twelfth share, and said he could prove that the will was false. In front of the magistrate he was questioned by Maximilla, and he claimed he could prove how the will was falsified. When Maximilla brought a charge of forgery against the writer of the will and her co-heir Proculus, and the case was heard, the prefect of the city declared the will was not false and the twelfth share of Maximilla was forfeit to the imperial treasury. The question is asked whether after these facts Aithales' freedom and *fideicommissum* are still owed. He replied that according to the facts given they were.

The background is that a person who unsuccessfully claimed, as accuser, that a will was false lost all benefits given to him under the will. Here the slave instigated one of the heirs to act as accuser and she failed to win her case. She lost her share of the inheritance, but the slave retained the benefits conferred on him. No doubt the reason for the latter part of the text is that the slave was not formally an accuser. The decision may seem remarkable, not so much because of the formalism of the reasoning behind it as because it shows an interpretation that unnecessarily favors a slave. Aithales does seem to have acted contrary to the spirit of the law.

Slaves could not be accusers in criminal law, either, and it must be for that reason that Hadrian enacted that complaints by slaves against mistreatment by their masters were not to be regarded as accusations. But slaves could act as *delatores* (informers) in cases of property owed in fiscal matters and also in crimes. Since delatores were paid a proportion of what was recovered, they were often disreputable, and penalties were established for laying false information. A slave could not be a delator against his master, even for a crime:

> *C.Th.*9.5.1.1 (Constantine, A.D. 320–23). Also in the case of slaves or freedmen who try to accuse or inform against their masters or patrons, the assertion of such atrocious audacity shall be repressed at the very outset of their offense, a hearing will be denied them, and they will be crucified.[24]

Later in the century an exception was made when the alleged crime was treason:

> *C.Th.*9.6.2 (Valens, Gratian, and Valentinian, A.D. 376). When slaves thunder forth as accusers of their masters, none of the judges is to await the outcome; it is settled that no inquiry is to be made, no investigation to be heard, but the authors of the wicked accusations are to be burnt along with the statements of the accusation, with all the instruments of the writing and of the intended criminal charge. We make an exception of attempted high treason, in which betrayal is honorable even for slaves, for this crime too is directed against *domini* [i.e., the emperors].[25]

Justinian's *Code,* though it reports the remainder of Constantine's enactment in *C.Th.*9.5, omits the section on slaves and freedmen recorded above.[26] The *Digest* tells us that slaves who act as delatores against their masters will not be heard and will be punished,[27] but other texts set out exceptions for treason, for suppressing wills that gave the slaves freedom, for certain public frauds and tax offenses, for forgery of coins, and for regrating.[28] These exceptions seem to have been earlier than the fierce constitution of Constantine; for instance, it was Marcus Aurelius and Commodus who laid down that slaves would be heard who charged the master with suppression of a will in which they were given liberty.[29]

Evidence from slaves was generally not admissible in civil cases, but when it was, it had to be taken under torture:

> D.22.5.22.1 (Arcadius, sole book on *Witnesses*). If the matter is of such a kind that we are compelled to admit as witness a gladiator or a similar person, the evidence is not to be believed without torture.[30]

As one might expect with such a rule, evidence was taken from a slave only if other evidence was insufficient, but there are indications that some other evidence had to exist.[31] We have no list of the types of situations in which a slave's evidence was permitted. A first case, obviously, is where the case involves an act of the slave himself; for instance, as a party to a contract:

> C.9.41.15 (Diocletian and Maximian, A.D. 294). There is no doubt that slaves can be interrogated about their own acts not only in a criminal case, but even in one involving money (for instance, when things are delivered by them to other people on account of deposit or loan for use or in other cases recognized by law).[32]

Other texts show a slave's evidence was permitted when ownership of him was disputed:

> C.9.41.12 (Diocletian and Maximian, A.D. 291). Whenever it is a question of ownership of slaves, if the truth cannot be uncovered by other proofs, the legal authorities approve the view that the slaves themselves may be examined, with torture.[33]

Similar rules applied when an inheritance was disputed,[34] although a constitution of Justinian himself shows that the law had once been far from settled:

> C.9.41.18 (A.D. 529). With regard to the torture of slaves forming part of an inheritance, we enact that slaves may be questioned only as to the corporeal things of the inheritance, and we make no distinction, as is found in earlier laws and constitutions, as to whether some question is raised between the heirs as to the right to the inheritance, or only as to

the corporeal things in the inheritance, or as to both of them. And it is permitted to bring only those slaves, whether they have been left in slavery or whether they acquire freedom through the last will of the testator, to the question with regard to things in the inheritance, who hold them for the sake of administration, so that of those things such as have been hidden are revealed. Prior to this, the oath decreed by us must be taken.

Unfortunately a further, fundamental text is ambiguous[35] and is hence here not translated. On one view it could mean that slaves' evidence can be given in cases involving money if otherwise the truth cannot be discovered. Or it might mean that in such cases involving money where slave evidence is permitted, it is admitted only if the truth otherwise cannot be uncovered. The latter interpretation seems much more likely in view of the other texts we have just looked at.

It is a matter for infinite regret that we do not have full information on the types of civil cases in which slaves could give evidence. The saddest gap is in the case of contracts made by a slave or in which slaves played an active role. We have express evidence—and that only from the third century A.D. on—for deposit and loan for use. We have already looked at C.9.41.15, but P.S.5.16.1 is possibly even more significant:

> Reasons of fairness indicate that a slave may be interrogated about his own actions: nor ought it be an obstacle to someone who lent or deposited something through a slave without a written document.

Both texts begin with an apparently general proposition, both give as illustrations loan for use and deposit, and in both the loan or deposit was made by—not to—the slave's master. Since these contracts were only imperfectly bilateral and in the normal instance only the depositor or the lender would be able to sue, the impact is that, so far as the texts are concerned, it is the slave's owner who is the plaintiff, and hence it is he who, in order to recover the value of his property, is ready to have his slave put to the torture. The slave is a witness for the master. In fact, P.S.5.16.1 expressly states that it is not to be to the master's disadvantage that when the transaction was handled by the slave no written document was prepared. We thus cannot tell whether a slave could be a witness against his master.

The opening of both texts, and the reasoning in *P.S.*5.16.1, would suggest that he could, and that he could also be a witness for other contracts, such as sale and hire, in which he was a party. But in fact we cannot tell. The point is of great practical importance. Slaves were extensively used in commerce. If the slave was always a competent witness, or even if he could be summoned only by his master and only in certain cases, but, of course, only under torture and only if there was otherwise not enough evidence, then he would have great incentive to make sure that there was always good evidence of the contract, that he was always scrupulously honest, and that the other contracting party was trustworthy. If the slave could not be called as a witness against his owner or only in certain limited cases, then the other party would have a practical burden placed upon him and would insist on a sufficiency of witnesses or written evidence. In any event, the outcome is that there is a gulf between the ease with which a contract could be made and the ease with which it could be proved.[36]

For slave's evidence in criminal cases it is sufficient to quote the long opening text of Ulpian in the relevant *Digest* title:

D.48.18.1 (book 8 on the *Duties of the Proconsul*). It is customary for torture to be applied to unearth crimes; but let us see when and how far this should be done. The deified Augustus laid down that one should not begin with the application of pain, and that reliance should not be placed entirely on torture, as is contained also in the deified Hadrian's letter to Sennius Sabinus. 1. The words of the rescript are as follows: "Recourse should only be had to the infliction of pain on slaves when the criminal is suspect, and is brought so close to being proved guilty by other evidence that the confession of slaves appears to be the only thing lacking." 2. The deified Hadrian wrote the same in a rescript to Claudius Quartinus; in this rescript he stated that a start should be made with the most suspect person and the man from whom the judge believes he can most easily learn the truth. 3. It is declared in a rescript issued by the deified brothers to Lucius Tiberianus that persons produced by the accuser from his own household should not be summoned to the torture, nor should it readily be believed that she whom both her parents are said to have treated as their beloved daughter is a slave. 4. The same emperors sent a rescript to Claudius Proculus that reliance should certainly not be placed on the torture of a single slave, but that the case should be examined by proofs. 5. The deified Antoninus and the deified Hadrian, to Sennius Sabinus, wrote in rescripts that, when slaves were alleged along with their master to have sent gold and silver out of the country, they should not be questioned about the master, in case they should of their own accord say something which would prejudice him. 6. The deified brothers wrote in a rescript to Lelianus Longinus that torture should not be applied to a slave belonging to an heir in matters concerning the inheritance, even though it had been suspected that the heir appeared to have sought the right of ownership over that slave by means of an imaginary sale. 7. It has very frequently been written in rescripts that a slave belonging to a municipality may be tortured in capital cases affecting the citizens because he is not their slave but the state's, and the same should be said of other slaves belonging to corporate bodies, for the slave appears to belong, not to a number of individuals, but to the body itself. 8. Should a slave serve me in good faith, even though I have not acquired actual ownership over him, it can be said that he should not be tortured in a capital case affecting me. The same applies to a freedman who serves in good faith. 9. It is also laid down that a freedman is not tortured in a capital case affecting his patron. 10. Nor indeed, as our emperor and his deified father wrote in a rescript, should a brother be tortured in a capital case affecting his brother, adding the reason that a person should not be tortured to give evidence against someone against whom he cannot be compelled to give evidence against his wish. 11. The deified Trajan wrote in a rescript to Sernius Quartus that a husband's slave could be tortured in a capital case affecting his wife. 12. The same emperor wrote in a rescript to Mummius Lollianus that the slaves of a condemned man, because they have ceased to be his property, can be tortured to give evidence against him. 13. The deified Antoninus Pius wrote in a rescript that if a slave is manumitted to avoid his being tortured, then, provided that he is not tortured in a capital case affecting his master, he can be tortured. 14. The deified brothers also wrote in a rescript that a slave who at the outset of a trial was the property of another, even if he subsequently becomes the property of the accused, can be tortured in a capital case against the latter. 15. If a slave should be said to have been bought invalidly, he cannot be tortured until it has been established that the sale was of no effect, according to a rescript of our emperor and his deified father. 16. Again, Septimius Severus wrote a rescript to Spicius Antigonus as follows: "Since information under torture ought neither to be obtained from slaves against their masters, nor, if this is done, should it guide the counsel of the person who is to pronounce sentence, much less should informations laid by slaves against their master be admitted." 17. The deified Severus wrote in a rescript that the confessions of accused persons should not be taken as equivalent to crimes established by investigation, if there were no proof to guide the conscience of the judicial examiner. 18. Although a certain person had been prepared to give the price of a slave, so that the slave might be tortured to give evidence against his master, our emperor and his deified father did not allow it. 19. Should slaves be tortured as participants in a crime in their own right, and confess something concerning their master to the judge, the deified Trajan wrote in a rescript that the judge should pronounce as the case requires. In this rescript it is demonstrated that masters may be injured by their slaves' confessions. But subsequent constitutions show a retreat from this rescript. 20. In a case involving tribute, in which no one doubts that the sinews of the state are concerned, the consideration of the risk which threatens capital punishment to a slave who is privy to a fraud corroborates his declaration. 21. The person who is going to conduct the torture should not ask specifically whether Lucius Titius committed a homicide, but in general terms who did it: for the former seems rather the action of someone suggesting an answer than seeking the truth. And so the deified Trajan wrote in a rescript. 22. The deified Hadrian wrote a rescript to Calpurnius Celerianus in these words: "Agricola, the slave of Pompeius Valens, can be interrogated concerning himself. If under torture he should say more than this, it is taken as evidence against the accused, not as a fault in the interrogation." 23. It is stated in constitutions that reliance should not always be placed on torture—but not never, either; for it is a chancy and risky business and one which may be deceptive. For there is a number of people who, by their endurance or their toughness under torture, are so contemptuous of it that the truth can in no way be squeezed out of them. Others have so little endurance that they would rather tell any kind of lie than suffer torture; so it happens that they confess in various ways, incriminating not only themselves but others also. 24. Moreover, you should not place confidence in torture applied to a person's enemies, because they readily tell lies. Not, however, that confidence in torture should be lost where enmity is alleged. 25. And it is only when the case has been investigated that you will know whether you can have confidence or not. 26. There is found in a number of rescripts the principle that, when someone has betrayed brigands, reliance should not be placed on the latters' accusations against those who betrayed them; but in certain rescripts that deal with the subject more fully, there is the proviso that you should neither make it a rigid rule not to rely on them, nor rely on them as you would in the case of other witnesses; but when the case has been examined it should be considered whether to trust them or not. For most people when they fear that others, on being arrested, may perhaps name them, are accustomed to betray those others first, as it were clutching at immunity for themselves, for it is not easy to believe those who inform on their own betrayers. But immunity should not indiscriminately be allowed to those making betrayals of this kind, nor should the counterallegations of those who say that they were accused solely because they themselves had handed over men be disregarded; nor should any argument that they put forward of falsehood or calumny deployed against them necessarily be treated as invalid. 27. If a person should confess to wrongdoing of his own accord, he should not always be believed; for sometimes people confess out of fear or for some other reason. There is extant a letter of the deified brothers to Voconius Saxa, in which is contained the principle that a man should be freed who had made a confession against himself but who, after condemnation, had been found to be innocent. Its words are as follows: "My dear Saxa, you have acted prudently and with the excellent motive of humanity in condemning the slave Primitivus, who had been suspected of fabricating a confession of homicide against himself for fear of going back to his master and was persisting in his false evidence, with the aim of interrogating the accomplices whom he had equally mendaciously declared himself to have, so that you could get a more reliable confession from them than his about himself. Nor was your prudent scheme in vain, since under torture it was established that they had not been his accomplices and that he had rashly told lies about himself. You can therefore set aside the verdict and by virtue of your office order him to be sold off, with the proviso added that at no time is he to return to the power of his master, who, we are advised, now that he has received compensation, will gladly be rid of such a slave." By this letter it is indicated that a seemingly condemned slave, if he be reinstated, will be the property of him who owned him before he was condemned. A provincial governor, however, does not have the power to reinstate a person whom he has condemned, since he does not have the power to revoke his own imposition of a fine. What, then, must he do? He should write to the emperor if at any time proof of innocence is subsequently established for a person who had appeared to be guilty.

Six

The Slave as Man: Slaves' Contracts and the Peculium

laves were very much used in commercial affairs and could enter freely into contractual relations.[1] Slaves (and sons, too) were particularly useful in this context at Rome, since, perhaps strangely, Roman law never developed the idea of direct representation. If Julius made a contract with Seius, who was acting under instructions from Marcus, and they were all free men, the contract firmly remained between Julius and Seius. Marcus could neither sue nor be sued on the contract. But slaves and sons, being in the power of the head of the family, could enter contracts that gave the paterfamilias the right of action. So far as entering a contract is concerned, a slave is in no different position from any free citizen, with two minor exceptions. First, in the oral contract of stipulation, which was the oldest Roman contract and which originally had to be made using the verb *spondere,* the form using *spondere* was restricted to Roman citizens.[2] But from an early date other verbs could be used to make the contract. Slaves could never make use of the form of stipulation using the verb *spondere,* but they could use all others. Second, in the subsidiary form of stipulation called *adstipulatio,* in which an alternative creditor was added to whom the debtor could make payment and obtain release from the obligation, the rights of this alternative creditor were purely personal; if he was a paterfamilias, the rights did not descend to his heir; if he was a son, the adstipulatio was suspended until he became independent; if he was a slave, the adstipulatio was void.[3]

But if the slave's contract gave his master full rights of action under it, it did not at civil law permit the master to be sued, and, of course, the slave himself, not being a person, could not be sued:

> D.44.7.14 (Ulpian, book 7 of *Disputations*). Slaves are bound by their delicts, and if they are manumitted they remain bound. On contracts, however, they are not bound at civil law, but by natural law their contracts both bind others and they are bound. And so if I pay to a manumitted slave who had lent me money I am released.

But the freed slave's obligation remained a natural obligation, and he could not be sued upon it unless the obligation was contracted with his peculium and he took the peculium into freedom with him:

> C.4.14.2 (Antoninus, A.D. 215). No action against you is available to your creditors who lent money to you while you were a slave, especially since you state that you did not receive a legacy of your *peculium*.

The master's freedom from liability on the slave's contract, far from being a benefit, must have been a great commercial hardship. No one would enter a contract with a slave in which performance was due from the slave's side but the contract could not be enforced, hence the commercial usefulness of the slave would be very limited. This difficulty was overcome to a very great extent by a series of praetorian actions, none of which is evidenced before the first century B.C., when they probably were introduced.[4] However, in this instance, as in delict, it was felt that a master should not be liable to an unlimited amount for his slave's activity. Hence in effect the rules still gave the master adequate protection and enabled him, when he so wished, to trade through the slave with limited liability.

The best known of these actions against the master is the *actio de peculio et in rem verso,* the action of the peculium and for property turned to account. Here the master was liable up to the value of the peculium at the time of judgement, and also to the extent that his estate had profitted. Evaluating the peculium could be a matter of some judgement:

D.15.1.9.2 (Ulpian, book 29 on the *Edict*). The *peculium* must be calculated after deducting what is owed to the master, because the owner is understood to have anticipated and sued his slave.[5] 3. Servius adds to this definition also if anything is owed to persons who are in the same power, since no one doubts that this also is owed to the master.

But on the basis of "first come, first served," debts owed from the peculium to other creditors could not be deducted.[6] However,

D.15.1.7.6 (Ulpian, book 29 on the *Edict*). But also what the owner owes him is in the *peculium,* for instance if he spent money on the latter's account and the master wished to remain his debtor, or if the master sued a debtor of the slave. . . . 7. But also if a fellow slave owes him anything that will be part of the *peculium,* provided that one has or will have a *peculium.*[7]

When a slave, with the knowledge of his master, traded with his peculium or a part of it, the creditor had a further remedy. Any creditor could ask for a *vocatio in tributum,* a call for bringing into contribution, in which the master was to divide the peculium or the relevant part among the creditors. This is in effect to treat the slave as bankrupt, with the master as administrator. If the master is fraudulent in the division, but only then, he becomes liable to the *actio tributoria:*

D.14.4.7.2 (Ulpian, book 29 on the *Edict*). If any one act fraudulently so that the bringing into contribution is not properly made, the *actio tributoria* is given against him, to make good the amount by which the sum brought in was less than he owed. This action punishes the fraud of the master. He is regarded as not bringing in properly, even if he does not bring into contribution at all. If, however, in ignorance of what goods the slave has he brings in too little, he is not regarded as having acted fraudulently, but if he does not bring it in once he has discovered the property, he is not now free from fraud.

This text also shows that the action lay for what should have been handed over, and this was the case even if the fund had been later diminished. The edict that set up the action spoke not of peculium but of *merx peculiaris,* wares forming the peculium. This term was the subject of interpretation:

D.14.4.1.pr. (Ulpian, book 29 on the *Edict*). The usefulness of this edict is not small, because the owner who otherwise in a slave's contracts is privileged (since, when the master is only liable on the *actio de peculio,* an estimate of what is owed to him is deducted from the *peculium*) is, nonetheless, if he knew his slave was trading with wares forming the *peculium,* called into contribution just like an external creditor. 1. Although the term "wares" is narrower, so that it does not apply to slaves who are fullers, tailors, weavers, or slave dealers, nonetheless Pedius writes in book 15 that it should be extended to all kinds of business. 2. We do not interpret "wares forming the *peculium*" as meaning *peculium,* because *peculium* involves the deduction of what is due to the owner, and wares forming the *peculium* bind the owner by the *actio tributoria* even if there is nothing in the *peculium,* provided the slave was trading with the master's knowledge.

Thus in determining the amount that could be recovered by the action, the owner was not allowed to deduct from the peculium sums owed to him. This may be considered an extremely small penalty to impose upon the owner, since the action lay only where the owner had been fraudulent, and, at that, in circumstances in which the fraud could be very easily concealed. The explanation is to be found when we look at the *actio de dolo,* the ordinary action for fraud, which also lay only for the plaintiff's loss. The answer is that the actio tributoria and the actio de dolo originally[8] lay only where there had been negotiations: the actions are basically contractual, and usually in such actions penal damages are not permitted.

A third remedy introduced by the praetor for contracts made by sons or slaves was the *actio quod iussu,* the action on account of authorization:

G.4.70. Above all, therefore, if the transaction was entered into with the authorization of the father or owner, the praetor has provided an action for the full amount against the father or the owner. And rightly, because whoever enters a transaction on this score seems to be relying more on the good faith of the father or master than on that of the sons or slave.

Where the master authorized the slave's contract, he was liable for the full sum involved. The text of Gaius makes it apparent that the relevant authorization was to the other contracting party, not to the slave. Authorization could take any form, and subsequent ratification was enough.[9]

These three actions were available against the paterfamilias equally whether the person who entered the contract was a slave or a son; their rationale was the inclusion of the slave or son within a family of which the head alone could own property, and so the acts of the slave or son were within limits treated as the acts of the paterfamilias. Two other actions, which rested on a very different basis, require mention. First, a person who establishes another in business as manager (*institor*) is liable to the full extent on trans-actions within the business by the *actio institoria*. And this is so whether the institor is one's son or slave, someone else's slave, or an independent, free person. Until late law, the principal could not sue on the contract of the institor where the institor was an inde-pendent, free man or another person's slave. To judge from the texts in the relevant *Digest* title (14.3), the institor was very commonly, or even most commonly, one's own slave. The texts here indicate the range of business activities that might be entrusted to a slave: to go abroad to buy goods, to be a funeral undertaker, to be a miller, to run an (olive) oil business, to be an innkeeper, a cattle or slave dealer, and so on.

The second similar action is the *actio exercitoria*, which was given against a person (*exercitor*) who appointed another, whether his own son or slave, another's slave, or an independent, free man, to run a ship:

> D.14.1.1.4 (Ulpian, book 28 on the *Edict*). The status of the ship master is of no relevance, whether he is free or a slave, whether he belongs to the person with authority over the ship, or to another. Nor is his age relevant; he who appoints him lays that to his own charge.

Liability to this action was determined by authority, not by knowledge:

> D.14.1.6.pr. (Paul, book 6 of *Short Notes*). If a slave acts as ship master without the authorization of his owner, then if the owner is aware of this he is liable as if on the *actio tributoria*, if unaware on the *actio de peculio*.

This rule was understood to mean that if the ship master engaged in acts that were unauthorized, the person who appointed him was not liable to other contracting parties:

> D.14.1.1.12. Therefore it is the appointment itself which lays down the terms that bind the contracting parties. Therefore if one put him in charge of a ship on the understanding that he was only to collect freight

but not that he was to let out space on the vessel (the *exercitor* himself letting out the space), the *exercitor* will not be liable if the ship master lets out space. . . . We may add that if the master was appointed so that he should hire out the ship for the carriage of certain goods, for instance vegetables or hemp, and he hires it out for marble or other material, the *exercitor* will not be liable.

We have seen how the master might be liable for slave's contracts. It remains in this chapter to discuss the peculium and what the slave might do with it. But the master's power to acquire possession and to usucapt through the slave's use of his peculium are best left to the next chapter.

The importance of the peculium for Roman slavery cannot be exaggerated. If much in Roman law and life can be said to dehumanize the slave,[10] the peculium did much to humanize him. There was no limitation on its size and virtually no legal limit on how it might be acquired. The law did not intervene to declare that certain kinds of gainful employment could not be exercised by slaves, and no limits were placed by law on slaves' education, whether for culture or for profit. Slaves might be high-income earners, and it was their peculium that could give them an important stake in society. The peculium was central to their self-respect. Though slaves, they need not be poor and could, indeed, hold slaves, even many slaves, of their own. The peculium gave them a direct personal incentive to work hard, and it urged masters to treat them with consideration. It was in the interest of masters and slaves alike that a master acquire the reputation for allowing his slaves to buy their freedom with the peculium.

Technically the peculium belonged to the slave's master, since a slave could own nothing. Nor indeed could the slave have lesser legal rights, such as possession:

D.41.2.49.1 (Papinian, book 2 of *Definitions*). Those who are in another's power can hold property forming part of a *peculium*; but they cannot possess it, because possession is not only a matter of physical fact but also of law.

Other disabilities affecting the slave might have an impact upon the peculium:

> D.3.3.33 (Ulpian, book 9 on the *Edict*). They say that a slave also and a son of the family may have a *procurator*. As to the son this is correct. As to the slave, we hesitate. We admit that someone may indeed look after the slave's affairs relating to the *peculium;* and Labeo is of the same opinion. But we forbid him to bring an action.

A *procurator* was a business agent, the term could be used of a general business agent or of someone appointed to do something specific, in particular, to conduct a lawsuit. The text shows, incidentally, that the peculium could be large—otherwise it would be pointless to indicate that the slave might have a general agent—and that the master would concede that in many ways it was a separate fund. This is true even of early times.

Very revealing is a provision of the Twelve Tables:

> *Epit. Ulp.* 2.4. A person ordered to be free under this condition: "If he gives my heir 10,000," even if he is alienated by the heir, will achieve his freedom by giving the money to the transferee. This the law of the Twelve Tables commands.

The precise sum to be given for liberty was, of course, not set in the Twelve Tables. Moreover, when a slave was given his freedom *inter vivos,* the peculium was automatically included in the gift, unless it was expressly excluded:

> D.15.1.53 (Paul, book 11 of *Questions*). If the *peculium* was not taken away from Stichus when he was manumitted it is regarded as granted to him. But he cannot sue debtors unless the actions were mandated to him.

The second sentence states what one would expect to have been the law; since the right to these actions would have been vested in the owner, it could not be transferred automatically.

> D.23.3.39.pr. (Ulpian, book 33 on the *Edict*). If a female slave gave property as if as a dowry to a male slave, then while their union was continuing they both acquired liberty and the *peculium* was not taken from them, and they then continued in that union, the matter is so regulated that if any corporeal things still existed that were given as if as dowry during their slavery, these are tacitly transformed into dowry.

Since Roman slaves could not marry, there could be no such thing as dowry. Roman marriage did not require any formalities but simply intention, and if the two freed slaves continued to live together they could be treated as married, and corporeal property given during slavery to the man as if it were dowry would, if it still existed, be treated as dowry.[11]

Masters might be less selfless in manumitting slaves by will; hence it is possibly not too surprising that manumission of a slave by will did not carry a presumption of a legacy of his peculium to him. There had also to be a legacy of the peculium, but whether there was or not could be a matter of interpretation:

> D.33.8.8.7 (Ulpian, book 25 on *Sabinus*). Sometimes even if there is not a legacy of the *peculium,* it will be treated as if there was a legacy, that is, in an instance of this kind: a person gave his slave his freedom if he rendered accounts, and if he gave the heirs 100. Therefore, our emperor together with his father issued a rescript that the *peculium* was not due unless as a legacy. "But," he said, "if the slave obeyed the conditions set out, our interpretation is that the testator wished him to have the *peculium*"; obviously from the fact that he ordered the slave to give 100 from the *peculium.*

The interpretation is generous and may be reasonable, but it is by no means necessary. The testator could well have intended to benefit the slave by giving him his freedom, but at little cost to the heir. The slave could have been expected to work harder to increase his peculium, and when the increase had reached 100 the slave could have been freed on delivering the sum to the heir. To judge from the legal texts, it was in fact very common to give a legacy of the peculium to slaves who were freed by will.

A peculium could only come into existence with the consent of the slave's owner, and an owner who was underage or insane could not consent.

> D.15.1.3.3 (Ulpian, book 29 on the *Edict*). Pedius says that even owners under the age of puberty are liable in respect of *peculium*, for the contract is not with the children themselves, and that the authority of the tutor be looked for. He also adds that a pupil may not constitute a *peculium* for his slave, even with the authority of the tutor.

But the slave of either an underage owner or one who was insane could have a peculium if, in the case of the former, the father had granted it, or if, in the case of the latter, if the lunatic granted it before his insanity or during a lucid interval. Why the peculium could not be granted with the authority of the *tutor* is a mystery,[12] especially since, as we have already seen, where the owner has limited legal capacity, it could be a great boon to have a slave through whom he could acquire. Perhaps the explanation is to be sought in a combination of legal logic and legal conservatism. The authority of the tutor was required for the creation of an obligation (which could make the pupil's financial position worse). The creation of a peculium was an act of administration entirely inside an owner's affairs and did not itself bring into being an obligation with a third party; hence there was no place for the tutor's authority. This understanding would be all the more natural if the rule developed at a time when there was no right of action against an owner on a slave's contract, even with the peculium.

But if the owner's consent to a peculium was necessary, it was not sufficient: the property had to be placed at the slave's disposal. The same rule applied to increases in the peculium from the master once it had been created:

> D.15.1.8 (Paul, book 4 on *Sabinus*). What the master wished to become *peculium* from his own property does not become *peculium* unless he delivered it or, when it was in the hands of the slave, he treated it as delivered; for the thing needs a natural delivery. On the other hand, as soon as he does not want the slave to have a *peculium,* the slave's *peculium* ceases to be *peculium.*

> D.15.1.4.1 (Pomponius, book 7 on *Sabinus*). This I believe to be true in this case, if the owner wished to release the slave from a debt the slave ceases to be debtor, even if the owner released the debt by a bare expression of intention. But if the master makes statements of account so that he appears to be in the position of a debtor to his slave when in fact he was not a debtor, then I hold the opposite opinion. For the *peculium* is to be increased by real transactions, not by words.

The debts mentioned in the text are, of course, debts between the master and the slave, not between an outsider and the slave.

Once established, the peculium will contain not only gifts from the master, but gifts from outsiders and gains from transactions. But it will not include profit from wrongdoing, whether against the owner or an outsider:

D.15.1.4.2 (Pomponius, book 7 on *Sabinus*). It appears from the above that the *peculium* is not what the slave has without the master's knowledge but what he has with his approval; otherwise even what a slave stole from his master would be *peculium,* which is not correct.[13]

What was included within the peculium might very often raise questions of fact, at times to be settled by interpretation:

D.15.1.25 (Pomponius, book 23 on *Sabinus*). Clothing begins to be part of the *peculium* if the master gave it that the slave might always want to use it, and the master handed it over on the understanding that no one else was to use it, and that the slave could keep it with a view to that use. But clothing that a master gave to a slave to use, not that he might always use it, but for a certain purpose at certain times, for instance when in attendance upon him or when serving him at table, that clothing is not *peculium.*

Of course, to give clothing which was needed to one's slave who did not have a peculium would not render that clothing peculium. Since a slave might hold in his peculium another slave, called a *vicarius,* complications might arise:

D.15.1.17 (Ulpian, book 29 on the *Edict*). If my ordinary slave (*ordinarius*) has *vicarii,* may I deduct from the *peculium* of the *ordinarius* what the *vicarii* owe me? And the first question is whether these *peculia* are counted in the *peculium* of the ordinary slave? And Proculus and Atilicinus hold that just as the *vicarii* themselves are in his *peculium,* so are their *peculia.* And indeed, what their owner, that is, my *ordinarius,* owes can be subtracted even from their *peculia;* but what the *vicarii* owe, only from their own *peculium.* But even if they owe something not to me, but to my ordinary slave, that may be deducted from their *peculium* as if it were a debt to a fellow slave. But what the *ordinarius* owes them is not deducted from the *peculium* of the ordinary slave, because their *peculium* is in his *peculium* (and this was the opinion of Servius), but their *peculium* (i.e., of the *vicarii*) will be increased, in my view, just as if an owner was in debt to his slave.

Acquisitions by a slave go into the peculium rather than into the master's general property if they are acquired through use of the peculium or an account of the peculium. The same applies in general to a gift, legacy, or inheritance to a slave.

D.15.1.7.5 (Ulpian, book 29 on the *Edict*). But also what is due to a slave under an action for theft or other action is counted in the *peculium;* likewise an inheritance and legacy, as Labeo says.

D.15.1.39 (Florentinus, book 11 of *Institutions*). The *peculium* also comprises what a person has saved through his frugality, or what he earned from anyone as a gift when that person wanted the slave to have it as his own property, as it were.

A text we examined earlier in this chapter (D.23.3.39.pr.) shows that what a female slave gave to a male slave as if it were dowry is treated as increasing the latter's peculium.

When we turn to the slave's right of alienation, we find that, for this, as one might expect, the master's authorization was necessary. This might be for a specific instance, or it might amount to a grant of *plena administratio* (full administration) or *libera administratio* (free administration). The extent of the grant was always in the hands of the owner, and it was always a matter of fact:

D.20.3.1.1 (Marcian, sole book on the *Action on Hypothec*). If a son in power or a slave pledges a thing in his *peculium* on behalf of another person, we must hold the thing is not pledged, although they have free administration of the *peculium*. For the power of making a gift is not allowed them, and they do not have free administration all the way. For it is a question of fact, if it is asked, how far they are thought to be permitted to administer the *peculium*.

The text, of course, also shows that the grant of full administration did not include the power of making a gift from the peculium, even indirectly. But it did include the right to alienate and to pledge where this was appropriate in the interest of looking after the peculium.

D.2.14.28.2 (Gaius, book 1 on the *Provincial Edict*). If a son or a slave made a pact that he himself would not sue, the pact has no effect. If, however, they made a pact with regard to a matter, namely that an action would not be brought for that money, the pact of theirs will be held good against the father or owner if they have free administration of the *peculium* and the matter about which the pact was made concerns the *peculium*. This must be qualified. For, since it is true, as Julian holds, that even if administration of the *peculium* to the greatest extent was granted him, he does not have the right to make a gift; then it follows that if the pact not to sue for the money was made in order to make a gift, the pact agreed on should not be ratified. But if he acquired something on account of the pact which was not less or even more, the pact should be ratified.

The incapacity of a son or a slave to make a gift must have been inconvenient for them in many contexts. But for the slave, above all it meant the slave could not make gifts from his peculium to someone who could use part of what he had received to buy the slave from his master and then free him.

Seven

The Master's Acquisitions through Slaves

The main end of slavery is to increase the master's satisfaction, whether he obtains this through pride in the augmentation of social prestige by conspicuous consumption, through the availability of personal services, or through economic betterment. The purpose of this chapter is to examine the legal rules—apart from those relating to the peculium—which enable the slave to improve the master's economic standing. The quality of these rules will have an important impact on the master's incentives to treat a slave well, on the slave's desire to be a "good" slave, and on the personal relationship between a slave and his master.

The chapter divides into three main topics: acquisition of ownership and possession through a slave; contracts by slaves and the appropriate action; and slaves as heirs or legatees.

The starting point must be that, as is the case of all domestic animals, the natural increase of slaves belongs to the owner, provided at least that his rights of ownership are untrammelled. Thus, children born to a slave mother, as we saw in the first chapter, belong to the mother's owner. But where the owner's right is restricted, an important legal distinction was drawn between slave babies and the offspring of other animals:

Cicero, *On the Ends of Good and Evil,* 1.4.12. There was a discussion among the leaders of the state, Publius Scaevola, and Manius Manilius whether a child should be included among the fruits. Marcus Brutus disagreed with them.

D.7.1.68.pr. (Ulpian, book 17 on *Sabinus*). There was an old question whether the child belonged to the usufructuary. But the opinion of Brutus prevailed, that the usufructuary had no right to the child: for a human being cannot be included in the fruits of a human being. On this account, the usufructuary will not have even a usufruct in him.

D.22.1.18.1 (Gaius, book 2 on *Everyday Matters*). But the child of a slave woman is not included in fruits, and so it belongs to the owner of the property: for it seemed absurd to include human beings among fruits, since nature procured the fruits of all things for the sake of human beings.

On one level the texts are primarily important for the light they cast on Roman lawmaking and the importance attached to it. Thus, the three jurists referred to by Cicero were all prominent politicians. Publius Scaevola and Manius Manilius both held the consulship, the highest public office, the former in 133 and the latter in 149 B.C. Marcus Brutus held the praetorship, the second highest public office in 142 B.C. Again, the issue was settled not by legislation or by any official intervention, but by a consensus of opinion among the jurists.

The question at issue involved a point in usufruct, life interest. There was no doubt that the general rule was that the usufructuary of a female animal, and not its owner, acquired the ownership of its young in exactly the same way as he acquired ownership of milk, wool, dung, and so on. But should the same rule apply to children born to female slaves? Scaevola and Manilius said yes; Brutus, whose view prevailed, said no. The significant issue for us is why this should be treated as a special case. Modern scholars provide basically three very different answers. The traditional answer is based on an idea of the Roman conception of fruits, namely, the return for which the bearer is usually kept.[1] Another view takes seriously what seem to be the arguments brought forward in two of our texts by the Roman jurists, and would base the decision on the concept of the dignity and worth of a human being, even when that being was a slave.[2] If this view is correct, then it would seem that for all the high moral tone, the Roman jurists did not necessarily have great concern for the well-being of the slave infant, since the natural result of the decision would be that the infant would be handed over to the true owner and thus separated from the mother, in whose absence the owner would be less likely to bring the child up and might even abandon it. A third modern opinion links the decision with the common opinion that in most cases the usufruct would be created by will, the usufruct being left to the widow, the property to the testator's children, who would include sons. A very likely father of a slave woman's child, it is then suggested, would be a free young male of the household, hence ownership of the child is being given, reasonably, to those among whom is the putative father.[3]

The basic picture of acquisition through slaves in classical law is set out by Gaius:

G.2.87. Therefore, whatever children in our power and slaves in our ownership receive by *mancipatio* or obtain by delivery, and whatever rights they stipulate for or acquire by any other title, they acquire for us. For a person who is in our power can have nothing of his own. And therefore if he is instituted heir he cannot accept the inheritance except by our command, and if he accepts it at our command the inheritance is acquired by us just as if we ourselves had been instituted heirs. And, of course, in the same way a legacy is acquired by us through them. 88. But we ought to keep in mind that if a slave is *in bonis* of one person, in full Roman ownership of another, he acquires from all sources solely for the person *in bonis* of whom he is. 89. Through those whom we have in our power we acquire not only ownership but also possession: we are regarded as possessing anything whose possession they have taken: on this account usucapion runs through them. . . . . 91. With regard to those slaves in whom we have only a usufruct, it is settled that whatever they acquire in connection with our affairs or through their own work is acquired by us, but whatever they acquire outside these grounds belongs to the owner of their property. Thus, if such a slave is instituted heir, or given a legacy or gift, he acquires not for me but for the owner of the property in him. 92. It is settled that the same rule applies when a person is possessed in good faith by us, whether he is a free man or the slave of another. For what has been held of a usufructuary is approved also for the possessor in good faith. Thus whatever he acquires outside of these two grounds belongs to him if he is free or to his owner if he is a slave. 93. But the possessor in good faith when he usucapts the slave, since he becomes owner in that way, can acquire for himself through him on all grounds. But the usufructuary cannot usucapt, first because he does not possess, but has the right of using and of taking fruits, second because he knows the slave belongs to another. 94. The question is raised whether we can possess and usucapt anything through that slave in whom we have a usufruct, since we do not possess him? Through a person whom we possess in good faith there is no doubt that we can possess and usucapt. In both cases I am talking according to the restriction just mentioned, namely if they acquire anything in connection with our affairs or through their work it is acquired for us. 95. From this it appears that we can acquire on no account through free persons whom we have neither subject to our power nor possess in good faith, similarly not through others' slaves in whom we do not have a usufruct or possess lawfully. And this is what is meant by the common statement that we cannot acquire through an outsider. The only doubt relates to possession whether we can acquire it through our general agent (procurator).

These texts of Gaius reveal the enormous importance of slaves for commercial and other acquisitions. Things which were classified as res mancipi, namely, slaves themselves, Italic land, cattle, horses, mules, asses, and rustic praedial servitudes, could only be transferred (as was discussed in chapter 4) by a formal ceremony called mancipatio which, among other essentials, required the physical presence of both the transferor and the transferee (or by a modified form of process, cessio in iure). Ownership of all other noncorporeal things could only be acquired inter vivos, by actual physical delivery (traditio).

Interesting questions arise as to the extent to which one could acquire through an intermediary. Acquisition of ownership by delivery to an extraneous free person has been studied relatively little, but it seems that the general position in both classical and Justinianian law was that one could acquire ownership by delivery to an outsider only if that person was merely an instrument and not also acting as agent.[4] When the principal had knowledge of the delivery to the agent, the position naturally was the same as where the intermediary was merely an instrument. Mancipatio made to an extraneous free person acting as an intermediary, whether simply as an instrument or as an agent, would not confer ownership on the principal.

As for acquisition of possession, Gaius, in 2.95, says generally that we cannot acquire through an extraneous free person. The only possible exception suggested by Gaius is that the question has been raised whether we can acquire possession through a procurator, a general agent. Gaius, as often, is a trifle old-fashioned; an earlier jurist, Neratius, claimed it was generally accepted that possession could be acquired through a procurator.[5] Only in late classical law was it accepted that one could acquire possession through any extraneous free person.[6] Contractual rights were not at all acquired in classical law through a free, independent intermediary, even if he were acting on an express mandate of the principal.

But acquisition through persons in the principal's power was a very different matter. We are, of course, here concerned with slaves. When mancipatio or delivery of res nec mancipi was made to a slave, the slave's master acquired ownership of the property. When a slave entered a contract, whether or not the contract was expressly in the name of the master, the master acquired all rights under the contract. In classical law the master acquired possession through a slave even when he was unaware of the delivery to the slave, but in the time of Justinian the master's unknowing acquisition of possession through a slave was restricted to delivery on account of the peculium. The whole question of the history of acquisition of possession through a slave has been much disputed among scholars,[7] with varying opinions on which of the conflicting texts have suffered change at the hands of Justinian's compilers. Conclusive proof for the state of classical law, it seems to me, comes from D.41.2.23.2 (Javolenus, book 1 of *Letters*):

> Likewise I ask, if I bind a free man in such a way that I possess him, do I possess everything that he possesses through him? He replied: if you bind a free man, I do not think you possess him; since that is the case, much less will his things be possessed by you. For the nature of things does not allow us to possess anything through a person whom I do not have in my power at civil law.

Obviously, there could be no possibility of a peculium here. If a master acquired possession automatically only of what the slave acquired through the peculium or when he learned of the slave's taking, the question in this text could not even have been raised. The same can be said of another question posed by Javolenus:

D.41.2.24 (book 14 of *Letters*). What without your knowledge your slave possesses by force you do not possess, because a person in your power does not acquire physical possession for you unawares, but lawful possession.

The situation of fact excludes both the use of the peculium and the master's knowledge. The discussion would be wholly pointless unless the master, without knowledge, automatically acquired possession through a slave acting lawfully but not using his peculium. In both classical and Justinianian law it seems that usucapion following upon a slave's taking began to run for the master only when the master learned of the taking, unless the taking was on account of the peculium.[8] Thus, the general picture.

What is immediately striking is that the configuration of the rules means that in commerce a slave can do much more for his master than an extraneous free person could. A Roman with mercantile interests in Alexandria would, from a legal point of view, be well advised to have a slave agent there rather than employ a free agent. The advantages of using the slave were particularly great for acquiring rights under contracts. From a modern perspective, what is possibly most surprising is not the ease of acquisition through slaves, but the problem of acquiring through extraneous free persons. Perhaps surprisingly, the Romans never developed direct agency. The Roman contract of mandate, where one person undertook to do something on behalf of another, did not directly give the principal an action against a third party who contracted with the mandatory. The contract was between the mandatory and the third party, and they alone could sue and be sued on it. Moreover, mandate was of necessity gratuitous. An arrangement that the agent would receive payment turned the contract into hire (*locatio conductio*), and there is not the slightest hint that an agent under locatio conductio who entered a contract even expressly on behalf of his principal acquired any rights at all for his principal on the contract against the third party. Yet for centuries before Justinian, the

Romans with their vast Empire had come into commercial contact with people who did use direct agency.[9] The concept was well known to them. The use that could be made of slaves, though it cannot be a full explanation, may help to explain why there was apparently little pressure to create direct agency.

The value of slaves in this context is all the greater because the Romans scarcely developed a contract of barter,[10] though barter was surely common even in transmarine trade. Moreover, the Romans never developed a general contract in writing; hence a written agreement could not make barter a contractual arrangement.[11] For legal effects to ensue, there had to be physical delivery to at least one of the parties, and this delivery could be to one party's slave.

As the passage from Gaius indicates, the general picture of acquisitions through slaves was subject to complications. Thus, we see from G.2.88 that, where there was a bonitary as well as a full civil law owner, all acquisitions went to the former. Again, the usufructuary acquired through the slave only what was acquired by means of the slave's labor or in connection with the usufructuary's affairs. The slave's owner acquired everything else. A similar division occurred when a slave was possessed in good faith. Where in fact the supposed slave was really a free man, what he acquired outside of the two causes was in fact acquired for himself.

The jurist Nerva the son (of the first century A.D. and probably father of the emperor Nerva) was responsible for the rule that an owner retained possession of a slave who had run away:

> D.41.2.3.13 (Paul, book 54 on the *Edict*). Nerva the son says that moveables, with the exception of man, are possessed only so far as they are in our keeping, that is so far as we have the power to take natural possession if we wish. For a herd so soon as it wanders off or a pot if it falls [from a balcony] and cannot be found, at once we cease to possess even though it is possessed by no one. The case is different for an object still in my keeping which cannot be found because it is still present and all that is lacking in the meantime is a diligent search.[12]

The principle for the ruling is not clear: For Ulpian it is because otherwise the slave might deprive the owner of possession of himself;[13] For Paul it is on the ground of utility—an argument used only when the decision is contrary to principle—so that prescription may continue to run;[14] for Nerva himself because the slave, unlike other self-propelling things, could have an intention to return.[15] For Nerva, as well as for others, the possession was lost as soon as someone else took hold of the slave.[16] But Nerva also held that one could not acquire possession of other things through a runaway slave.[17] Later jurists disagreed.

A rather special case is represented by the institution of a slave as heir and by a legacy to a slave. The institution of one's own slave as heir is not relevant to this chapter because, since the institution had to be accompanied by freedom, there was no acquisition through such a slave. But the legal possibility of instituting another person's slave as heir is rather astonishing. There was no obstacle to this, provided that the slave's owner had the capacity to take:

> D.28.5.31.pr. (Gaius, book 17 on the *Provincial Edict*). We can institute as heirs slaves no less than free men, provided of course they are slaves of persons whom we could institute heirs, since the relationship of testamentary capacity with slaves was introduced from the person of the masters.

As is not uncommon with Roman legal texts, the jurist shows little concern for the plausibility of his argument. Gaius's point is that institution of another's slave is possible because it benefits his owner. The general rule was that only Romans and members of Latin city states could be heirs under a Roman will; hence the possibility of instituting another's slave is an interesting concession. Before we consider it further, a few words should be said about heirs in general.

Roman heirs fall into three main classes: *necessarii heredes* were slaves freed and instituted by the testator, and they had no power to refuse the inheritance; *sui et necessarii* were the sui heredes of the deceased—that is, those who became free of all paternal power on the death—and they also had no power to refuse; *extranei heredes* were outsiders (including other people's slaves). In time, a limited power of refusing the inheritance was given to sui heredes. Not only did Roman heirs take all benefits belonging to the inheritance, they were also responsible for all debts, even if the debts greatly exceeded the benefits. Hence it was a serious business for an *heres extraneus* to accept an inheritance, and, not surprisingly, acceptance by a slave (not belonging to the deceased) required his master's consent. Until the inheritance was accepted it belonged to no one.

To judge from the legal texts it was by no means uncommon for a Roman citizen to appoint another's slave as his heir or leave him a legacy. The institution of the slave is in effect institution of his owner, hence the rule that the institution is valid only if the owner is a person who has legal capacity to become heir. The inheritance goes to the owner at the time of the acceptance of the inheritance, not at the time of the testator's death:

> J.2.14.1. A slave instituted heir by his own master, if he remains in that condition becomes free and a necessary heir. But if the slave was manumitted by the master while the latter was alive, he can accept the inheritance at his own option, because he is not a necessary heir, since he does not receive both the inheritance and freedom under the will. But if he was alienated, he will enter on the inheritance at the request of his new owner, and therefore the owner becomes heir through him. For if he has been alienated he can become neither free nor the heir, even if he had been instituted heir with the gift of freedom. The owner who alienated him is regarded as having taken from him the gift of freedom. Also another person's slave who has been instituted, if he remained in that condition, should accept the inheritance at the request of his owner. But if he was alienated by him, whether during the lifetime of the testator or after his death, but before the slave enters upon the inheritance, he enters at the request of the new master. But if he was manumitted before he entered upon the inheritance, while the testator was alive or dead, he can enter the inheritance at his own choice.[18]

The inheritance cannot be accepted without an order from the master, and this order must precede the entry: ratification will not suffice:

> D.29.2.25.4 (Ulpian, book 8 on *Sabinus*). The command to enter from one who has a person in his power is not similar to the authority of a tutor, which may be interposed when the transaction is complete, but it must precede, as Gaius Cassius writes in his second book on the civil law: and he thinks it may be made by intermediary or by letter.

The explanation is that entry was an *actus legitimus* (an "act in the law"), and as such could not be subjected to a suspensive condition.[19] The master's order was essential for the entry; hence, if it was not given before entry and ratification was permitted, an actus legitimus would in fact have been subjected to a suspensive condition. But the master's command, not itself being an actus legitimus, could be made in any way at all:

D.29.2.93.1 (Paul, book 3 of *Opinions*). The more correct view is that a dumb father or master, if he is not mentally defective, may order his son or slave who has been instituted heir to enter upon the inheritance so that the benefit may rightly come to him.

But the order must be specifically for the particular inheritance, and the owner must know whether the gift is of whole or of part of the inheritance, whether the slave was instituted heir or was only a substitute heir.

D.29.2.25.5. But may the order be general, "Whatever inheritance has been left to you," or special? And the better opinion is, as Gaius Cassius writes, that he must give a special instruction.

D.29.2.93.pr. (Paul, book 3 of *Opinions*). Whenever a father instructs a son to make entry, he must be certain whether his son is heir in whole or in part, as institute or substitute, by a will or an intestacy.

What is difficult to understand in all this is why an outsider should even wish to appoint another person's slave as his heir. The institution does not benefit the slave, and it is not easy to see an advantage for the master. If the testator had wanted to benefit the slave, it would have been more satisfactory to appoint the master heir on condition that he manumit the slave within a certain time, or else to leave the master a legacy on the same condition. If the testator had wished to benefit the master, it would have been simpler to leave the inheritance to him: the slave could only enter if the master had the appropriate testamentary capacity. It was dangerous, too, to institute the slave, since he might die or be alienated by a master unaware of the benefit that could come to him. In either eventuality the former master would have no rights to the inheritance. P. F. Girard suggested two ways in which the institution might benefit the slave, three ways the master.[20] First, the slave would benefit if he acquired freedom before the testator died. This is true, but how could a testator estimate this possibility? Indeed, if the master suspected that his slave was instituted heir he would have a good reason for not freeing him. Second, the successive owners of the slave, if they knew of the institution, would have an extra incentive to keep the slave alive. Yes, but it is hard to envisage a testator who was so anxious to keep another's slave alive that he was indifferent as to who eventually took his inheritance, but who at the same time took no other positive step to benefit the slave's position. For the master, says Girard, the first advantage is that, whereas the sale of an eventual right to an inheritance (that is, a sale before the death of the testator) was void, the master could sell the slave who would eventually become heir. But however theoretically sound this might be, it would in practice be impossible for the owner to sell the inheritance indirectly. No one would pay highly for the slave on this basis, not only because the transaction was risky, since the slave might die before the testator, but also because there was absolutely nothing to prevent the testator from making an entirely new will. The second advantageous case for the master, says Girard, is that if a master who was instituted personally died before acceptance, his heirs would not take, but they would if the master was instituted through the slave and the master died. But, of course, it might be the slave who died, and then neither the master nor his heirs would get anything. To avoid the danger, the testator would be better advised to institute the master as heir, and then substitute to him the person of his second choice. The third beneficial case, especially in early law, is that if the free heir was insane or a pupil, he could not accept the inheritance until he became sane or left childhood, but if the institution was of his slave, the slave could enter at the command of his master's curator or tutor. There seems to be no objection against Girard on this point, but this type of case seems too limited to account for the law's permission of this kind of institution or of its apparent popularity.

Two details of instituting another's slave demand to be noticed. First, acquisition through a slave's entry was not regarded as acquisition through the slave's work, hence if he was serving a master in good faith but in reality he was free or another's slave, the inheritance did not belong to his apparent master, but to himself or his true owner:

D.41.1.19 (Pomponius, book 3 on *Sabinus*). What a free man in *bona fide* servitude to me acquired through his own work or my property belongs to me without doubt according to Aristo. But what someone gave him or he got through a business transaction belongs (says Aristo) to himself. But, he says, an inheritance or legacy is not acquired by me through him, since it results neither from my property nor from his work—for there is no work with regard to a legacy, a little for an inheritance, since it was entered upon by him (which was once doubted by Varius Lucullus); but the better view is that I do not acquire even if the testator wished it to come to me. But even if he does not at all acquire for him, if the intention of the testator appears clearly, then the inheritance must be handed over to him. But Trebatius says that if a free man serving in good faith enters upon an inheritance at the order of the person he was serving, he himself becomes heir, and it does not matter what he thought, but what he did. Labeo takes the different view if he had acted from necessity; but if he himself had wished to enter, then he becomes heir.

We should look at a striking text that, according to Buckland, shows that the master and the slave might at times be treated as different persons.[21]

D.29.4.25 (Celsus, book 16 of *Digest*). A person to whom his own slave was substituted ordered the slave to enter upon the inheritance. If he did this in order not to pay out legacies, he will pay under both counts; because he is heir and because he possesses the inheritance by right of substitution when the main ground of the will was passed over. But his Falcidian right is preserved.

By the *lex Falcidia* of the very end of the Republic, heirs were always entitled to at least one-quarter of the estate. If more than three-quarters of the estate was left as legacies, the legacies were cut down *pro rata*. The purpose of the lex was to persuade the heir to accept the inheritance. Thus, the owner was instituted heir with legacies left from him; to the owner one of his slaves was substituted heir with legacies left from him but to lesser value. To avoid paying out the larger amount, the owner refused the inheritance for himself, but ordered his slave to accept as substitute. Pomponius decided that both sets of legacies were due up to the limit fixed by the lex Falcidia. Despite Buckland, this cannot be a decision where master and slave were treated as different persons. If it had been, then either the master accepted in his own name and had to pay out the relevant legacies, or (when he refused) the slave became heir and the legacies from him were due. Rather, the decision must be purely pragmatic. The master must not benefit from his wiliness in refusing for himself; but neither must the legatees from the slaves have their reasonable expectations dashed.

Eight

Punishment of the Slave

With the exception of punishment, whether by the master or by the state, we have now looked at all of the major topics of slavery as they are set out in the legal sources. The legal sources reflect the concern of the lawmakers, not directly that of the rest of the society. This is particularly true of the Roman jurists whose writings appear in the *Digest*. They are interested in the legal rules and how they should be interpreted, not with their importance, their frequency of use, or how far they were ignored in practice; they are not even interested in difficulties of proof. No distinction appears between their treatment of real cases and hypothetical cases, and usually it is not possible to know in which of these categories a case falls. This must always be borne in mind when drawing conclusions for societal conditions from the juristic treatment. But, of course, the legal treatment must in general bear considerable traces of public concern. The jurists themselves are members of society and will share the interests of their compatriots; rules of no great social importance are, overall, less likely to receive extended treatment. As for the law itself, absence of a rule may mean that the social problem never arose or that the problem was considered to be one not suitable for treatment by law.

The starting point for an examination of the master's rights to punish slaves in the Republic can well be W. W. Buckland's famous book *The Roman Law of Slavery*. He says: "During the Republic there was no legal limitation to the power of the *dominus; iure gentium* his rights were unrestricted. It must not, however, be supposed that there was no effective protection. The number of slaves was relatively small, till late in that era, and the relation with the master far closer than it afterwards was. Moreover, the power of the Censor was available to check cruelty to slaves, as much as other misconduct."[1] Others, too, write of censorian intervention as protecting slaves against cruel masters. Thus A.H.J. Greenidge simply writes: "The slave was unprotected by the civil law, and until the introduction of the *Lex naturalis* into Roman jurisprudence, there were no rights of men as such which might safeguard him. But the cruel punishment of a slave was visited from the earliest times by the censors."[2]

But how effective was the protection of the censors? It should be stated immediately that this protection is mentioned by Dionysius of Halicarnassus in his comparison of Athens and Rome. At Athens, he says, any man was free to act inside his own home as he liked. At Rome, in contrast, every house, and even the bed chamber, was open to the authority of the censor: "For the Romans believed that neither should a master be cruel in the punishments doled out to his slaves, nor a father be too severe or gentle in training his children, nor a husband unjust in his partnership with his wife, nor children disobedient to their aged parents," and so he goes on.[3] It is not obvious that much weight should be attributed to this passage. In the first place, Dionysius provides no specific examples of censors punishing cruel masters. We need take out of the passage only that censors could punish cruel masters—which no one would doubt—not that they actually did so. Second, how much Dionysius really understood of the work of the censors may be doubted. He mentions, as if open to the censors' authority, children who were disobedient to their parents. But the nature of the censorian mark of disapproval was such that it could be used only against a paterfamilias, a male who had no living male ancestor to whose power he was subject.[4] Thus, children who disobeyed their aged father could not be disciplined by the censors, and any mark of censorian

116

disapproval would be put against the aged father, who was held responsible for the children's behavior. At the very most, sons in power might be rebuked by the censors. If Dionysius could be misleading here, it is not clear that he would necessarily know much about censorian disapproval of cruel masters. Perhaps more significant than this weak passage of Dionysius is the total silence of the Roman writers on any specific instance of censorian intervention against a cruel master, a silence that can scarcely be the result of chance.[5] The Romans relished stories about rigid censors, so the silence here is particularly noteworthy.

The issue, of course, is not whether the censors could, or even occasionally did, punish cruel masters. It is whether the censors' power could and did effectively check cruelty to slaves. The answer must be a resounding no.

First, censors were appointed only at intervals of four or five years, five being more usual, and at times there were much longer gaps. The maximum period for which they could hold office was fixed according to tradition in 434 B.C. by the *lex Aemilia* at eighteen months.[6] This means that, in general, for three and a half years out of every five there were no censors to disapprove of cruelty. Only the most notorious instances would even have a chance of being remembered.

Second, slaves had no access to censors or other elected public officials or judges. They had no standing and no legally recognized avenue of approach to anyone in authority. No machinery was created by which their complaints could be heard. In addition, they were in the physical control of the master, who could mistreat even more those who might be tempted to complain of ill treatment. If any complaint was to be made to the censors, it would have to be made by a citizen. It seems impossible to believe that such complaints could ever have been frequent or meaningful. To begin with, unless the cruel treatment of a slave was public and blatant, another citizen would have had no direct experience of it. Class or group solidarity, a component of every society, would also make it rare for one citizen to inform on another for mistreatment of his slaves. However kind and close to his own slaves a citizen might be, outside of his family his ties were with the other citizens (especially those of similar wealth and social standing), not with the slaves of other people. This is so, even though gossip from one household might spread, via slaves, to another. Further, unless the cruelty was public, evidence of it would be almost impossible to obtain. Slaves would not be questioned by the censors about their masters, and if they were, their word would be suspect.

Three apparently unconnected details will illuminate how improbable it is that the censors' *regimen morum* could have been effective in controlling cruelty to slaves.

The first relates to the lex Aelia Sentia of A.D. 4, in the reign of Augustus. Gaius, in his *Institutes* (1.13), tells us:

> By the *lex Aelia Sentia* it is provided that slaves who have been branded or who on account of wrongdoing have been questioned under torture and who have been found guilty of that wrongdoing or who have been handed over to fight in the arena with sword or with wild beasts or who have been cast into a gladiatorial school or prison, and are subsequently manumitted, whether by the same master or another, become free men of the same status as surrendered enemies.

Under the statute, some freed slaves are not to acquire citizenship but are to be placed in the lowest possible category of free non-citizens, and these slaves are those who have been severely punished by their master or tortured by the state. But the statute draws an express distinction: where the freed slave had been questioned under torture he now has this lowly status *only if he had been found guilty;* where the freed slave had been put in bonds or branded by his master he now acquires this status *whether he had been at fault or not.* Whatever else we may conclude from the distinction, there could be no greater evidence of a lack of interest in the rightness or wrongness of a master's savage treatment of his slave. To his dying day the slave, if freed, would carry the burden of his punishment, merited or not. The law dates from the early Empire, but it is unlikely to incorporate changed attitudes to cruelty by masters. D.20.1.27 (Marcellus, book 5 of *Digest*) also illustrates this lack of concern. A master pledged a slave, then put him in chains for a very trivial offense (as we are expressly told). It is made obvious that for the jurist the slave's market value has been reduced. The sole question is whether the creditor has an action for the harm done to his security.[7]

The second detail—which I have never seen mentioned—encompasses both the Empire and the Republic. To the best of my knowledge, not one single surviving legal text refers in any way whatever to sexual abuse of slave children by a master. This cannot be accidental and requires explanation. The leading alternatives must be that such abuse did not occur or was rare, or that it was not a matter that interested the law or the jurists. General knowledge of human nature might suggest that the former alternative is implausible. This is supported by D.47.10.25 (Ulpian, book 17 on the *Edict*), which gives the master the action for damage to property against a person who raped (or seduced?) his immature virgin slave girl. But if sexual abuse of slave children by the master did not excite juristic comment, it seems unlikely that mistreatment of slaves by masters would often in the Republic attract the moral indignation of the censors. I hope to show later in this chapter that legislation that protected slaves, when it came, was not primarily moral in character.

The third instructive detail is found in the well-known, even famous, text of Seneca, *On Anger*, 3.40.1–3. Its significance remains, even if it is a moral, rhetorical piece of fiction invented by Seneca or another.

> To chide a person who is angry is only to incite his rage. You should approach him with various gentle appeals, unless you are such an important person that you can reduce his anger just as the Deified Augustus did when he was dining with Vedius Pollio. One of his slaves had broken a crystal cup. Vedius ordered him to be seized and to be put to death in an unusual way. He ordered him to be thrown to the huge lampreys which he had in his fish pond. Who would not think he did this for display? Yet it was out of cruelty. The boy slipped from the captors' hands and fled to Caesar's feet asking nothing else other than a different way to die: he did not want to be eaten. Caesar was moved by the novelty of the cruelty and ordered him to be released, all the crystal cups to be broken before his eyes, and the fish pond to be filled in.

Apparently Vedius Pollio believed masters could treat a slave as they wished, and he did not expect to be interfered with for feeding a slave to his lampreys. Augustus's response was extralegal but was permitted by his position of power. Augustus, it may be recalled, was later to restore the censorship.

Restrictions on masters gradually made their way into the law, even though into the time of Justinian the master's right to kill a slave remained.

> J.1.8.1. Therefore slaves are in the power of their masters. This power indeed comes from the law of nations; for we can see that among all nations alike masters have power of life and death over their slaves, and whatever is acquired through a slave is acquired for the master. 2. But nowadays, it is permitted to no one living under our rule to mistreat his slaves immoderately and without a cause known to the law. For, by a constitution of the deified Antoninus Pius, whoever kills his slave without cause is to be punished no less than one who kills the slave of another. And even excessive severity of masters is restrained by a constitution of the same emperor. For when he was consulted by certain provincial governors about those slaves who flee to a holy temple or to a statue of the emperor, he gave the ruling that if the severity of the masters seems intolerable they are compelled to sell their slaves on good terms, and the price is to be given to the owners. For it is to the advantage of the state that no one use his property badly. These are the words of the rescript sent to Aelius Marcianus: "The power of masters over their slaves should be unlimited, nor should the rights of any persons be detracted from. But it is in the interest of masters that help against savagery or hunger or intolerable injury should not be denied to those who rightly entreat for it. Investigate, therefore, the complaints of those from the family of Julius Sabinus who fled to the statue, and if you find they were more harshly treated than is fair or afflicted by shameful injury, order them to be sold so that they do not return to the power of the master. Let Sabinus know that, if he attempt to circumvent my constitution I will deal severely with his behavior."

The text is taken from Gaius, who, however, does not quote the rescript[8] and who gives a rather different explanation for it: "for the same reason prodigals are interdicted from the administration of their property."

The reasons given for restricting the masters' power are revealing. Not a word is said about the well-being of slaves, and this is true also for the texts that refer to earlier restrictions. But Gaius makes a correlation with prodigals. They are interdicted from administering their property in the interest of the relatives who will inherit their estate and who will suffer if it is squandered. Likewise, masters who mistreat their slaves reduce their value, and this should be prevented in the interest of their relatives. The rescript of Antoninus Pius that is thought worthy of quotation by Justinian in the *Institutes* and again in the *Digest* actually stresses that masters should have unlimited power over their slaves, and the claim is that it is in the interest of masters that help against savagery should not be denied to those who entreat for it. Presumably "masters" here means the slave-owning class in general rather than the individual masters who abuse their slaves. If this is so, then Antoninus Pius is referring to an eternal tension in slave-owning communities—between protection of slaves from cruel masters and the authority of masters— which will be discussed shortly.[9]

There is, incidentally, an interesting sidelight on the rescript of Pius. Protection was afforded a mistreated slave if he fled to the statue of the emperor. But it was standard practice in buying a slave to demand a guarantee that he had not fled to the statue.[10] Such a slave was obviously thought to be not the kind one wanted to buy.

The passage from Justinian's *Institutes* gives the main points; we must nonetheless set out the details of the historical development.

The first known step is probably by a *lex Petronia,* of unknown date but before A.D. 79, since we have a record of it from Pompeii, which was destroyed by the eruption of Vesuvius in that year:

> D.48.8.11.1 (Modestinus, book 6 of *Rules*). When a slave has been given to the beasts without the approval of the judge, not only is the person who sold liable to the penalty, but so is the purchaser. 2. After the passing of the *lex Petronia* and the *senatus consulta* pertaining to it, the power was taken from masters to hand over at their own discretion slaves to fight with wild beasts. If the slave has been brought before a judge and the complaint of the owner is just, the slave may be handed over for that punishment.

The way the text is written makes it plain that the main thrust of the statute (of which we do not have the wording) was against masters handing over slaves to fight wild beasts of their own volition. The reference to relevant senatus consulta suggests that the statute left much still to be done on the subject, and that is rather confirmed by D.18.1.42 (Marcian, book 1 of *Institutes*):

> Neither directly nor through agents may owners sell even their criminal slaves to fight with wild beasts. And this is the import of a rescript of the deified brothers.

Perhaps this later rescript was useful because the statute had not made it plain that it was intended to apply also to slaves who were obviously guilty of a serious crime.

Near in time to the lex Petronia was an edict of the emperor Claudius:

> Suetonius, *Deified Claudius,* 25.2. When certain men were exposing their sick and worn-out slaves on the island of Aesculapius because of the trouble of treating them, he declared that all who were exposed became free, nor were they to revert to the master's control if they recovered. But if anyone wished to kill rather than expose he would be liable to the charge of murder.

A text in the *Digest* (40.8.2) and one in the *Code* (7.6.1.3) confirm that the ruling was by an edict, and the *Code* text tells us that if the slave recovered, his status was that of a Latin. Neither of these texts mentions the island of Aesculapius in the Tiber—Aesculapius was the god of medicine—and nothing in the text of Suetonius shows that the edict was restricted to exposure there. Indeed, any such restriction would surely have defeated the purpose of the edict. It is sometimes suggested[11] that Suetonius, not being a precise writer, may have given too early a date for the rule that it was murder to kill one's own slave. Perhaps the reason for this view is the contrast between the two parts of the edict: one that permits a master to allow a slave to die; one that punishes severely a master who kills a slave. But there is no psychological conflict: the absence of a duty to provide care in order to keep alive may easily coexist with a duty not to kill. Interestingly, the main provision of the edict does not restrict the master's power to do what he wants with his slaves; a note is struck that is similar to the opening words of the rescript of Antoninus Pius.

Domitian (Emperor, A.D. 81–96), notorious for his cruelty, did restrict the power of masters:

Suetonius, *Domitian,* 7. He forbade the castration of males; he restricted the price of eunuchs who remained in the hands of slave dealers.

D.48.8.6 (Venuleius Saturninus, book 1 of the *Duties of the Proconsul*). Under the *senatus consultum* which was issued when Neratius Priscus and Annius Verus were consuls, a person who handed over his slave to be castrated is fined one-half of his property.

The senatus consultum seems to date from A.D. 83. The severity of the penalty may suggest that castration was very profitable and the practice not easily eradicated. It is not easy to tell whether the senatus consultum should be linked with the provision of Domitian recorded by Suetonius. Imperial concern with the issue continued, and Hadrian declared that the castration of a slave or free person, whether with his consent or against his will, whether on account of lust or to make a profit, was to be brought within the scope of the *lex Cornelia,* that is, it was to be treated as murder:

D.48.8.4.2 (Ulpian, book 7 on the *Duty of the Proconsul*). Likewise the deified Hadrian issued a rescript: "It is laid down that males are not to be castrated, and those who are found guilty of this crime are to be liable to the penalty of the *lex Cornelia* and their property is to be justifiably claimed by my treasury. And also slaves who castrate males are to suffer the supreme penalty. And those who are liable for this offense, if they were not present, then a verdict is to be given in their absence, as if they are liable to the *lex Cornelia.* Clearly if those who suffered this injury cried out, the governor of the province should hear them. But likewise the castraters should be punished even if these who lost their manhood are silent: for no one ought to castrate a free man or a slave whether he permitted it or it was against his will. But if anyone acts against my edict the penalty is capital, even for the doctor who did the cutting, and likewise for a person who gave himself voluntarily for castration."[12]

Hadrian also punished general cruelty toward a slave:

Coll.3.3.4. Also the deified Hadrian expelled from the country for five years a certain matron called Umbra, because for very slight reasons she had treated her slave women in a most atrocious fashion.

We have already quoted the rules of Antoninus Pius on the treatment of slaves. The direction the law was taking is apparent, but how much still had to be done is well shown by a rescript of Alexander Severus:

C.3.36.5. It was in the power of your husband to change what, when angry, he provided in his will against his slaves, that one be kept perpetually in chains, another be sold for export. Thus if he moderated his fierceness with mercy (which, even if it is not proved by writing, nothing prevents being shown in other ways, especially when their merits are later revealed so that the owner's anger might be reduced), the judge in the action for dividing an inheritance follows his latest intention.

This is a big concession, since the will is usually taken as conclusive of the testator's intention and provisions cannot be disturbed at all by other evidence.[13]

Half a century later we have a rescript of the emperors Diocletian and Maximian from the year 285 addressed to a soldier:

Coll.3.4.1. When you maintain that your slave died as a result of serious illness, your innocence—whose truth you maintain—does not permit the accusation of calumny to be clearly seen, because of your immoderate punishment.

The background to this rescript is easy to reconstruct. A soldier had punished his slave very severely, and the slave died. A free man complained of this and probably had an action brought against the soldier for the killing the slave. The soldier insisted that the slave had died as a result of illness, and the killing—possibly not thoroughly investigated—was not proved. The soldier now wants to sue the other person by the action for calumny, usually given for actions brought in bad faith. Diocletian refuses, because the brutal punishment by the soldier prevents the innocence of his claim being seen. Diocletian's insistence on the innocence, as claimed, of the soldier seems a trifle ironic.

There was no dramatic change bettering the slave's lot when the Empire became Christian.[14] Constantine, the first Christian emperor, decreed:

C.Th.9.12.1 (A.D. 319). If a master beat a slave with a rod or whip or put him in chains to guard him, and the slave dies, the master need have no fear of prosecution. Distinctions of time and questions of interpretation are abolished. He should, of course, not use his right immoderately, but he will be charged with murder only if he killed the slave intentionally, by a blow from the fist or a stone, or, by using a weapon, he inflicted a lethal wound, or ordered him to be hanged by a noose, or by a wicked order instructed that he be thrown from a high place, or administered the virus of a poison, or tore his body by public punishment, that is, by tearing through his sides with the claws of wild beasts, or by burning him with fire applied to his limbs, or if, with the savagery of monstrous barbarians, he forced the slave to leave his life almost in the tortures themselves, with the destroyed limbs flowing with black blood.

The rescript is retained in Justinian's *Code,* 9.14.1. "The claws of wild beasts" appear to have been instruments of torture which were made out of metal. The reference to "distinctions of time" and so on, suggests that there had been earlier rulings that drew distinctions based on the space of time that elapsed between the punishment and the death. A decade later the emperor issued another rescript on the subject:

> *C.Th.*9.12.2. Whenever such chance accompanied the beatings of slaves by masters that they die, the masters are free from blame who, while punishing very wicked deeds, wished to obtain better behavior from their slaves. Nor do we wish an investigation to be made into facts of this kind in which it is in the interest of the owner that a slave who is his own property be unharmed, whether the punishment was simply inflicted or apparently with the intention of killing the slave. It is our pleasure that masters are not held guilty of murder by reason of the death of a slave as often as they exercise domestic power by simple punishment. Whenever, therefore, slaves leave the human scene after correction by beating, when fatal necessity hangs over them, the masters should fear no criminal investigation.

These two rescripts are at times cited to demonstrate that the law was becoming more humane to slaves.[15] Against that view it is enough, I believe, to point to the rescript of Antoninus Pius which has already been quoted. But C. Dupont, for instance, draws two distinctions.[16] First, under the rescript of Antoninus, she says, a master is guilty who kills his slave without cause. Under the rescript of Constantine the question is different; namely, it is enough to know if the master used or did not use punishments that were prohibited and barbarous. Second, she says that the main innovation of Constantine lies in the use of the phrase "he will be charged with murder." She admits that under Antoninus the master who killed without cause suffered the same penalty as one who killed another's slave, and that the owner of a slave whom someone had killed could ask for a criminal prosecution that carried the capital sentence. But, she says (with others), the courts were indulgent in such cases, more so than if the victim had been a free man.

We may dispose of part of Dupont's second point fairly quickly. It is reasonable to assume that the courts would be more indulgent to the killer where the victim was a slave, but we cannot tell whether this attitude changed once the Empire became Christian. In other respects, the two rescripts of Constantine and the interpretation of them that has just been described raise serious questions for Roman law in general, not all of which can be answered.

We may begin with the assertion that for the first time it has become murder to kill one's slave. The earlier rescript of Antoninus does not name the offense, and whether or not it was called murder does not seem of great significance. What matters is the treatment of the crime and its punishment. We are told that the penalty is the same as for killing another's slave. What is in issue cannot possibly be the civil action for damages: the master cannot be suing himself. Hence it must be the crime, for which the punishment is capital. If this argument is correct, then Constantine's rescripts do not necessarily seem to mark an advance toward a more humane regard for slaves. Actually Suetonius, discussing the edict of the emperor Claudius, does in fact say *caedis crimine teneri* ("liable to the charge of murder") of masters who kill their slaves.

Second, Dupont's argument in favor of the increased mildness of the law toward slaves under Constantine is that the question is whether or not the master used forbidden means of punishment. This is inaccurate, even if we consider only *C.Th.*9.12.1. According to the rescript, two questions must be asked. First, were prohibited modes of punishment employed? If the answer to that question is positive, but only then, does one ask the second question, did the master kill intentionally? Thus, for criminal prosecution of the master, Constantine in *C.Th.*9.12.1. is adding an extra requirement.

A third problem is whether the two rescripts of Constantine *C.Th.*9.12.1 and *C.Th.*9.12.2 are to be taken as a unitary statement of the law, or whether the latter may be regarded as a substantial modification. *C.Th.*9.12.2 could be read as excluding all criminal investigation where a slave dies at the hands of his master, even when there was evidence of a deliberate killing, or it could be understood as being restricted to deaths following upon permitted punishment. The rescript does not say that there will be an investigation if forbidden punishment is applied and the slave dies. The problem for removing the ambiguity comes from the nature of imperial rescripts as a legal source. Until rescripts were issued as a collection, as in the *Theodosian Code,* it was not easy for persons other than the addressee to know their contents. This was so even when, as here, the rescripts were apparently issued to public officials.[17] The office of Maximilianus Macrobius, the addressee of *C.Th.*9.12.2, is unknown, and we cannot tell whether he could have had knowledge of the contents of *C.Th.*9.12.1. Even if it can be assumed that he had, we still would not know whether in the later rescript Constantine was adopting a modified stance. Since the compilers of the *Theodosian Code* were instructed by Theodosius II in 429 to collect all general laws enacted from the time of Constantine and were expressly told to retain obsolete laws (*C.Th.*1.1.5), we cannot tell even for the early fifth century whether or not the two rescripts are thought to be in harmony. It may be significant that *C.Th.*9.12.2 with its—at least apparently—more lenient view toward masters does not reappear in Justinian's *Code.* It is certainly significant that *C.Th.*9.12.1 does at *C.*9.14.1, and that the rescript of Antoninus Pius is also retained, even more prominently, in *J.*1.8.2, and in *D.*1.6.2. For Justinian, at any rate, the rescript of Antoninus Pius and the first rescript of Constantine are to be regarded as being in harmony.

A final question, perhaps the most important of all, admits of no easy answer. How, in practice, were cruel masters to be brought to justice? There is an inevitable tension, in states where the slave population is extensive, between protection of the slave from cruel masters and the authority of masters. Protection of slaves is not just a humanitarian issue: it is also important for the state. The rescript of Antoninus Pius claims that it is in the interest of slave owners— presumably as a whole—that cruelly treated slaves have the possibility of relief. Otherwise slave frustration may lead to slave revolt.

On the other hand, masters would find it intolerable if slaves could continually challenge their authority by threatening to haul them into court for misbehavior. The Roman solution was to deny the slaves access to the courts except where the action was a claim that a slave was really free and (by the rescript of Hadrian in *Coll.*3.34) where the slave's complaint was that he had been castrated. In addition, as we have seen, if the slave took refuge at a shrine or imperial statue, then by the rescript of Antoninus Pius the slave's complaint would be investigated, but the slave was not regarded as an accuser. If the slave was killed, obviously he was in no position to bring a criminal charge against his master; nor—at least from the time of Constantine under *C.Th.*9.5.1.1 (which was quoted in chapter 5)—could his fellow slaves be of assistance, since it was forbidden under pain of death to act as informer against one's master. Nor is much improvement to be found in the next half-century of Christianity, as is shown by *C.Th.*9.6.2 (A.D. 376) (which was also quoted in chapter 5). Consequently, masters who killed a slave deliberately would be brought to justice only if fellow citizens laid complaint or if there was a spontaneous investigation by the authorities. Neither practice seems likely to have been common.[18]

Later legislation regulated the use of imperial statues or temples as places of refuge not just for slaves.

> *C.Th.*9.44.1 (Valentinian, Theodosius, and Arcadius, A.D. 380). We allow those persons who took refuge at the statues of the emperors, whether to avoid danger or to create ill will, neither to be removed by anyone nor to depart of their own accord before the tenth day; provided that if they had certain reasons for which they had to flee to the images of the emperors they will be protected by law and the statutes. But if they should be revealed to have wished to create ill will by their tricks against their enemies, an avenging sentence will be pronounced against them.[19]

*C.Th.*9.45.4 (A.D. 398) and *C.Th.*9.45.5 (A.D. 431) show that Christian churches have taken over the role of sanctuary from pagan temples; they also lay down standards of behavior both for the fugitive and for any pursuer.

Leo, who was emperor from 457 to 474, addressed a rescript to the people:

C.1.4.14.pr. Let no one attempt to expose a slave or free person to
unchastity or to be a member of a theatrical orchestra or any manner of
actor. If a slave is prostituted, a successful action for liberty may be
brought without cost by anyone approaching the magistrates or the very
reverend bishops of the place.

And Justinian provided[20] that a free or slave woman could not be
compelled to remain an actress or theater musician against her will.
The stage was looked upon as a very degrading occupation, hence
the concern that Justinian's wife, the empress Theodora, had been
an actress or, it is reported, worse.[21]

Punishment of slaves by the state may be dealt with under five
heads: crimes which might be committed equally by slave or free
man; crimes which might be committed only by slaves or with the
involvement of slaves; crimes for which a slave could not be tried in
the ordinary way; the defense of superior orders; and the murder of
an owner of slaves. The last head is the subject of the next chapter.

The basic general proposition for a criminal action when a slave
was the defendant was that the same proceedings and rules applied
as when the defendant was a free man:

D.48.2.12.3 (Venuleius Saturninus, book 2 of *Public Actions*). If the
defendant is a slave, then, in accordance with the *senatus consultum*
issued when Cotta and Messala were consuls, the same must be observed as would be the case if he were free.

The *senatus consultum Cottianum* dates from A.D. 20. But the basic
proposition was not without exception:

D.45.16.6 (Paul, sole book on *Adultery*). Domitian issued a rescript to
the effect that what is said about holidays and the pardoning of
defendants does not apply to slaves who when they are accused are
ordered to be held in chains until the action is complete.[22]

The import of the rescript is clarified by *D.48.3.2.pr.* (Papinian,
book 1 on *Adultery*):

If a slave is charged with a capital crime, then it is provided by statute
that a guarantee should be given by the owner or an outsider that he will
be produced in court, and security is to be taken. But if he is not
defended, he is ordered to be thrown into public fetters to plead his case
in chains.

From this second text we learn what could also be known from other texts, that a slave charged with a crime can be defended by his master, or, failing this, by an outsider.[23] Security for his production in court is to be given. But if no one defends the slave the trial still goes on and, contrary to the usual rule that a slave can take no part in an action, he is allowed to defend himself. But since no security for his appearance in court is forthcoming, he is kept in chains. The master's failure to defend the slave is not taken as proof of guilt. The point, then, of the first text is that a slave who is not defended is not included in a general pardon issued on holidays to persons awaiting trial.[24]

The ambiguities inherent in the treatment of slaves who are thought to have committed a crime are well brought out in D.48.2.5 (Ulpian, book 3 on *Adultery*):

> There is no doubt that slaves can also be accused of adultery. But those who are forbidden to accuse free men of adultery likewise are forbidden to accuse slaves. But as the result of the rescript of the deified Marcus, the master can institute an accusation even against his own slave. Therefore after this rescript the necessity of accusation of his own slave falls on his owner: but a lawfully married woman may take advantage of prescription.

Since slaves could not marry, and sex between slaves was not contrary to law, the adultery here is with a free woman. Certain disgraced persons or persons of low standing could not bring criminal charges, and Ulpian tells us the restriction is the same whether a suspected adulterer is free or is a slave. How far this rule was conceived to be in the slave's interest or in the interest of the free woman is an open question. The background to the second part of the text is that, under legislation of Augustus, a husband whose wife was taken in adultery was bound to make an accusation or be himself guilty of the crime of *lenocinium* (pandering). The rescript of the emperor Marcus Aurelius (161–80) was, it seems legitimate to assume, issued in response to a request on a particular instance. Where the male adulterer was a slave belonging to the husband, the husband was nonetheless bound to bring the accusation against the slave. Adultery was a crime that prescribed, but the passage of time did not run to the advantage of a slave accused, though it would for a woman in a civil law marriage.

The trial of an accused slave took place where the crime was said to have been committed:

D.48.2.7.4 (Ulpian, book 7 on the *Duties of the Proconsul*). The same emperor issued a rescript that slaves are to be punished where they are said to have offended; and their master, if he wishes to defend them, cannot have the case moved to his own province but ought to defend there where they offended.

This rescript is by Antoninus Pius (138–61) and gives a ruling on jurisdiction that does not differ from that for free men.

Some crimes could be committed only by a slave or with the involvement of a slave. Thus, from at least the time of Constantine, cohabitation of a slave and his female owner carried a death penalty for both of them.[25] Likewise, at least for some periods, it was a capital offense for a slave, aware of his status, to offer himself for military service;[26] under Diocletian and later, it was also capital for a slave who had not received the right of gold rings (i.e., become a knight) or been restored to free birth to aspire to become a decurion (i.e., a local councillor);[27] and under Theodosius and Valentinian, a slave who dared to bring certain types of lawsuits against the imperial treasury was to be thrown to the flames or to the wild beasts.[28] More interesting for us perhaps are the crimes committed by a slave in running away and by those who helped him.

As we have seen, jurists disagreed as to whether it was theft to persuade a slave to run away. But under Constantine it was a serious offense to retain a runaway slave.

C.6.1.4.4 (A.D. 317). Whoever harbors a fugitive slave in his house or on his land without the knowledge of his owner must return the slave and one like him or twenty gold pieces. But if he harbors him a second or third time, in addition to him he must deliver to the owner two or three others or the foresaid valuation for each of them. . . . 2. But if he is unable to pay the said penalty, punishment will be meted out to him according to the discretion of a competent jurist.

Likewise it was a crime to support in bad faith a runaway in a claim of liberty.[29] The senate made provision to search a person's land for runaways:

D.11.4.1.1 (Ulpian, book 1 on the *Edict*). The senate decreed that runaways should not be admitted into woodlands nor protected by bailiffs or procurators of the possessors, and they laid down a fine. To those, however, who within twenty days either returned the fugitives to the masters or produced them before the magistrates they gave pardon for their previous conduct. Further on in the same *senatus consultum*, immunity is granted to one who, within the fixed times, handed over to the owner or magistrate fugitives found on his land. 2. This *senatus consultum* also granted a soldier or civilian access to the land of senators or civilians for the purpose of searching for a runaway (provision was also made previously for this by the *lex Fabia* and a *senatus consultum* made when Modestus was consul); a letter addressed to the magistrates should be given to those wishing to search for runaways, and a fine of one hundred gold pieces is established for magistrates who, on receipt of such a letter, do not help the searchers. The same penalty is established for those who prevent their own property from being searched. There is also a general letter of the deified Marcus and Commodus in which it is declared that governors, magistrates, and police must assist an owner in searching for fugitives, both that they return those who are found and that they punish those on whose property they hide, if a crime is involved.

There were some crimes for which slaves could not be tried in the ordinary way:

D.48.2.12.4 (Venuleius Saturninus, book 2 on *Public Actions*). Slaves can be the defendants under all statutes with the exception of the *lex Julia* on private violence, because those condemned under that statute are punished by the confiscation of a third part of their property, a penalty which cannot fall upon a slave. The same must be said about other laws in which a pecuniary penalty is inflicted or even a penalty affecting the status—such as banishment—which is not suitable for punishment of slaves. Likewise the *lex Pompeia* on parricide should not apply, since the first chapter deals with those persons who kill parents, relatives, or patrons, which, so far as the words are concerned, cannot apply to slaves: but since nature is the same, they are similarly punished. Likewise, Cornelius Sulla declared that a slave was not to be a defendant under the *lex Cornelia* on insult and assault; but a harsher penalty threatens him in the extraordinary procedure.

Similar rules applied in other criminal actions where the penalty for a free man was a fine.

Since a slave was bound to obey his master, he had a defense to a charge where the offense was not atrocious.[30]

D.44.7.20 (Alfenus, book 2 of *Digest*). A slave does not always in all cases obey his master with impunity, for example, if the master ordered the slave to kill a man or steal from someone. Therefore, although it was at the order of his master that a slave committed piracy, an action ought to be given against him after he has been freed. And he ought to pay the penalty for whatever he did by force, where the force was connected with evildoing. But if some quarrel arises from a lawsuit and controversy, or some force was used for the sake of retaining a right, and villainy was absent from these occasions, then it is not right for the praetor, since the slave acted at the order of his master, to give an action on that account against him when he was free.

Alfenus was active in the first century B.C. It is significant that the text opens as if in most situations the slave who obeys his master in wrongdoing will be free from liability. Alfenus appears to understand the weakness of the slave's position, but the substance of the text is much harsher. Other texts show that sometimes the defense operated to reduce the penalty.[31]

Nine

Senatus consultum Silanianum

The *senatus consultum Silanianum* could have been included in the preceding chapter, but I prefer to treat it separately for a number of reasons. First, it is not easy to regard as "punishment" the official torturing and execution of persons who have done nothing. Second, I wish to approach this topic differently, quoting extensively the relevant *Digest* title and also, for one particular case, a passage from Tacitus. The examination of much of a title will reveal Roman juristic techniques. No title is better adapted, moreover, to show the power of purely legal reasoning, the quasi-autonomous status of law, the basic inhumanity of a slave state occasionally illuminated by human sympathy, and a brilliantly elegant legal solution to a social problem.

The senatus consultum Silanianum dates from A.D. 10 and primarily declares that when a master is murdered, all the slaves who lived under the same roof are to be subjected to torture and then condemned to death.

D.29.5.1 (Ulpian, book 50 on the *Edict*). Since otherwise no home can be safe, unless slaves at the risk of their own lives are compelled to guard their masters as much from members of the household as from outsiders, *senatus consulta* have been introduced on the public questioning (torturing) of the household slaves of those who have been killed. 1. The term "master" covers the person who has ownership, even if someone else has the usufruct. 2. One who possessed a slave in good faith is not included within the term "master," nor is he who had only the usufruct. 3. A slave given in pledge is to be regarded, so far as the debtor's death is concerned, in all ways as if he had not been given in pledge. 4. In the term "slave" are included even those who were left by a legacy under a condition, for in the meantime they belong to the heir; nor does the coming about of the condition, so that they cease to belong to the heir, have the effect that they are not regarded as his in the meantime. The same must be said about the *statuliber*. . . . 6. It must be held that one who has a share is included within the term "master." 7. Within the term "master" is included a son of the family and other children who are in paternal power: for the *senatus consultum Silanianum* applies not only to the heads of families but also to their children. 8. What are we to say if the children are not in paternal power? Marcellus expresses doubt in the twelfth book of his *Digest;* I think the term is to be taken in a wider sense so that it applies also to those children who are not in power. 9. I do not think the *senatus consultum* applies to one who was given in adoption, although it does to one who has been adopted. . . . 11. If a son or daughter has been killed, torture will not be applied to the slaves of the mother. . . . 13. Likewise Scaevola says that the view should be firmly maintained that where a son is appointed heir and the son is killed before the inheritance is accepted, torture and execution should be applied to those who were unconditionally left as legacies or manumitted: for although if he lived and became heir they would not be his slaves, still in the case where he died and therefore legacy and freedom failed there will be scope for the *senatus consultum*. . . . 17. Labeo writes that in the term "killed" are included those who have been slaughtered by force or a wound as, for instance, where their throats were cut, they were strangled or thrown from a rock or struck by the fist or a stone or killed by some other weapon. 18. But if someone has been done away with, for example, by poison or even some other means which usually kills secretly, punishment for his death will not be a matter for this *senatus consultum*. The reason for this is because the slaves are to be punished on the ground that they did not bring help to their master whenever they could have given him help against violence and did not do so. But what could they have done against those who ambushed a man by poison or in some other way? . . . 24. Likewise it should be made plain that there will be no torturing of the household unless it is clear that someone was killed; for the *senatus consultum* to apply it must be established that he was carried off by a crime. . . . 26. However, this *senatus consultum* always punishes those who were under the same roof, but not those who were not under the same roof but in the same district, unless they knew of the crime. 27. But let us see how "under the same roof" is to be interpreted, whether within the same walls or beyond that yet within the same living room or bedroom or the same house or the same park or the whole country house? And Sextus says that it has often been decided that whoever was in such a place that they could hear cries, they are to be punished as if they were under the same roof, though some have a stronger, others a weaker, voice and everyone cannot be heard everywhere. . . . 32. A slave who is under puberty or a slave girl who is not yet capable of sexual intercourse will not be treated in the same way: for their age deserves to be excused. . . . 34. But slaves are excused who gave help and did not act fraudulently. For if someone pretended to give help or gave it as a mere gesture, his behavior will do him no good.

Only fr. 13 requires elucidation. The situation is that the will becomes effective only when the heir instituted in it actually agrees to accept the inheritance. In this case, the heir under the will is also the person who will be heir on intestacy if the will fails (through no fault of his). In the will some slaves are legated unconditionally and others are freed. If the heir accepted the inheritance under the will, then the slaves will be regarded as having belonged to the legatees or as having been manumitted from the moment of the testator's death; and they will never have been the property of the heir. But the heir was killed before he accepted the inheritance. Hence the will fails and, with it, the legacies and the manumissions; hence from the moment of the testator's death they belonged to the inheritance; and hence the senatus consultum applies to them.

D.29.5.3.2 (Ulpian, book 50 on the *Edict*). If a husband at night killed inside the bedroom his wife sleeping with him, or a wife her husband, the slaves will be free from the penalty of the *senatus consultum*. But if they had heard and had not brought help they will have to be punished, not only if they were the wife's own but even if they were the husband's. 3. But if a husband killed his wife caught in adultery then because he is excused the slaves will be released not just of the husband but also of the wife if they did not offer resistance to a master satisfying his just resentment. . . . 8. A deaf slave is also to be counted among those who are helpless or among those who are not under the same roof because, as they hear nothing because of the distance, he hears nothing because of a defect. . . . 16. Punishment must also be applied to those slaves who were manumitted by will, just as to slaves. . . . 18. It is provided in the edict that no one shall knowingly and with wrongful intent see to the opening, reading out, and copying of what has been left by way of testamentary disposition of him who is said to have been killed before the torturing of that household under the *senatus consultum* has taken place and the execution of the guilty.

Slaves manumitted by will should become free at the moment of the testator's death; hence, logically, they should not be within the ambit of the senatus consultum, but by fr. 16 the purpose of the senatus consultum is given precedence. It is partly to avoid this obvious torturing and execution of a free man that the senatus consultum orders the will not to be opened until afterward, though a further reason is that the person named as heir in the will would have a financial motive to restrain justice. If the heir accepted the inheritance before the torturing and execution of the slaves, he forfeited his right to the inheritance.[1]

The one case to be reported dates from A.D. 61, and a notable feature is the fellow feeling of the common people for the slaves. The jurist Cassius, who plays such a prominent role, is one of the most celebrated.[2]

Shortly afterward, a slave of his killed the prefect of the city, Pedanius Secundus, either because the slave had been refused his liberty after a price had been agreed or because he was consumed by love and could not tolerate his master as a rival. But when, in accordance with ancient custom, the whole household of slaves which had resided under the same roof were to be executed, a crowd gathered to protect so many innocent lives and rioted. The senate house was besieged. Inside there, too, there was feeling against extreme severity, but the majority believed nothing should be changed. Among those, Gaius Cassius spoke as follows: "Senators, I have often been here when new decrees of the senate were requested against established rules and laws of our ancestors. I did not oppose them, not because I had doubts about the superiority in all things of the old order and that changes were for the worse, but lest I seemed, by excessive ardor for ancient custom, to boast about my calling, the law. At the same time I did not wish, by frequent contradiction, to destroy whatever estimation I had, so that it might remain intact if ever the state needed my advice. That time has come today, when a former consul is murdered inside his house, ambushed by a slave. No one stopped him or betrayed him, although the *senatus consultum* has not been repealed which threatens the whole household with execution. Grant them impunity, if you like! But then whom will his rank protect, when it did not save the prefect of the city? Whom will the number of his slaves protect when four hundred did not protect Pedanius Secundus? To whom will the household bring aid if they do not avert danger from us in fear for their own lives? Or, as some do not blush to fabricate, did the killer avenge his wrongs because he was negotiating about his patrimony or his ancestral property? Let us decide straightaway that the master was justifiably killed!

May I refute arguments though wiser men have settled the matter? But even if we were now deciding the issue for the first time, would you believe a slave intended to kill his master and did not utter one threatening word and said nothing rashly? Even assuming he concealed his intention, he acquired a weapon without the knowledge of others, he passed the watch, opened the bedroom door, carried in a light and committed the murder, all without anyone knowing? There are many advance signs of a crime. If slaves give them away we can live in safety, though one among many, because of their anxiety; and if we must die we will not be unavenged on the guilty. Our ancestors distrusted their slaves even when they were born on their estates or in their own home and experienced the kindness of their masters. But now our households are international, they contain foreign religions or none. You can restrain this scum only through fear. But, it is said, even innocent people will die. Yes, but when in a defeated army every tenth man is flogged to death, even the brave have to draw lots. Every great example contains some evil, but individual wrongs are weighed against the public good."

No one dared speak against the opinion of Cassius, but many cried out in pity against the number or the children or the women and the undoubted innocence of so many. But those who decided for execution prevailed. But a threatening crowd, which gathered with rocks and torches, prevented the order from being carried out. Then Nero rebuked the crowd by edict and lined with guards the whole route along which the condemned were led to punishment. Cingonius Varro proposed that also the freedmen who had been under the same roof should be deported from Italy. But this was forbidden by the emperor lest ancient custom, which was not tempered by mercy, should be aggravated by savagery.

Notes

Preface

1. *An Introduction to the Study of the Roman Law* (Boston: Little, Brown, 1854), p. 129.
2. See the forthcoming work of Michael H. Hoeflich, *Roman Law and Anglo-American Jurisprudence.*

Introduction

1. On the fear of slaves see, e.g., F. Favory, "Clodius et le péril servile: fonction du thème servile dans le discours polémique cicéronien," *Index* 8 (1979): 173 ff, and the works he cites.
2. *Laws,* book 6, 777c.
3. *Conquerors and Slaves* (Cambridge: Cambridge University Press, 1978), p. 9.
4. Direct information on professional and businesslike work of slaves is notoriously scanty, but Suetonius, in *De grammaticis et rhetoribus,* gives us biographies of famous grammarians and teachers of rhetoric. Of the former, fifteen or sixteen out of twenty-one, of the latter, one out of five were slaves or freedmen: see, e.g., J. Kolendo, "Intellectuels et couches serviles: le cas des grammairiens chez Suétone," *Index* 8 (1979): 214 ff.
5. Though blacks were not particulary singled out as the victims of racial prejudice: see, e.g., F. M. Snowden, *Blacks in Antiquity: Ethiopians in the Greco-Roman Experience* (Cambridge: Harvard University Press, Belk-

nap Press, 1970), pp. 169 ff; idem, *Before Color Prejudice* (Cambridge: Harvard University Press, 1983).

6. But see, above all, Hopkins, *Conquerors,* and the works he cites.

Chapter 1 Enslavement

1. *Slavery,* p. 1. For a general account of slave law at Rome see O. Robleda, *Il Diritto degli Schiavi nell'antica Roma* (Rome: Gregoriana, 1976).
2. *D.*50.17.202.
3. *D.*1.5.4.1.
4. *J.*1.1.pr., from the first book of Ulpian's *Regulae* (Rules) (*D.*1.1.10.pr.).
5. *J.*1.1.1, from the same book of Ulpian (*D.*1.1.10.2).
6. *J.*1.1.3, also from the same book of Ulpian (*D.*1.1.10.3).
7. *D.*40.13.1.pr.
8. *D.*40.12.7.2; 40.12.33.
9. *D.*40.12.14.pr.; see Lenel, *Edictum,* p. 387.
10. See A. Watson, *Law Making in the Later Roman Republic* (Oxford: Clarendon Press, 1974), pp. 31 ff; Kaser, *RPR,* 1:292.
11. *D.*4.4.9.4.
12. See, e.g., *D.*4.4.9.2, 5.
13. By *adrogatio,* the form appropriate to a person who was not in paternal power.
14. For what follows see now also P.R.C. Weaver, "The Status of Children in Mixed Marriages," in *The Family in Ancient Rome,* ed. B. Rawson (Ithaca: Cornell University Press, 1985), pp. 145 ff.
15. Emperor, A.D. 117–38.
16. Which cannot be the *senatus consultum Claudianum.*
17. Emperor, A.D. 69–79.
18. *P.S.*2.21a.1; *C.Th.*4.12.2; 4.12.3; 4.12.4; 4.12.7.
19. *C.Th.*4.12.2.
20. See, above all, R. Reggi, *Liber homo bona fide serviens* (Milan, Giuffrè, 1958).
21. See G. Härtel, "Der *favor libertatis* im *Imperium Romanum,*" *Index* 5 (1974–75): 281 ff.
22. See D. Daube, "Greek and Roman Reflections on Impossible Laws," *Natural Law Forum,* 1967, pp. 1 ff.
23. Buckland, *Slavery,* p. 401.
24. The word *liberi* may be translated as "children" or "free men"; in the context, the latter seems preferable.
25. *D.*21.2.13.
26. This might be a dangerous thing to do, since the texts come from different historical times.

27. Other minor instances where a slave woman may give birth to a free child will emerge in other contexts.
28. Exactly what constituted being a *fur manifestus* was never quite settled, not even for the time of Justinian: *D.*47.2.3; *h.t.*4.
29. Aulus Gellius, *Noctes Atticae (Attic Nights)*, 11.18.8.
30. Aulus Gellius, *Noctes Atticae*, 20.1.46.47.
31. *D.*49.16.4.10.
32. *C.*8.51.3.
33. Penal slavery will be dealt with in a later chapter.
34. See, e.g., Watson, *Persons*, p. 229.
35. *D.*37.14.5; Suetonius, *Claudius*, 25.1.
36. Tacitus, *Annales (Annals of Rome)*, 13.26.27.
37. Arranged in historical order: *C.*6.3.2; 6.3.12; 7.16.30; 6.7.2; 6.7.3; 6.7.4.
38. Strangely, Buckland (*Slavery*, p. 424) claims that *D.*4.2.21 is the only *Digest* text not so far mentioned that refers to this power; but he then proceeds to discuss others.
39. For a full discussiion of the text see now Watson, *Persons*, pp. 162 ff. On Cicero, *pro Cluentio*, 59.102, see Watson, *Persons*, p. 159.
40. *D.*49.15.24;. *C.*7.14.4.
41. See, e.g., L. Amirante, *Captivitas e Postliminium* (Naples: Jovene, 1950), pp. 32 ff.
42. See, e.g., Amirante, *Captivitas;* for early Rome see, e.g., A. Watson, *Roman Private Law around 200 B.C.* (Edinburgh University Press, 1971), pp. 56 f.
43. See also *D.*24.2.1.
44. *D.*49.15.8; 49.15.14.1.
45. *C.*8.50.(51).1; *D.*38.17.1.3; 49.15.9; 49.15.25.
46. See, e.g., A. Watson, "*Captivitas* and *Matrimonium*," *T.v.R.* 29 (1961): 243 ff at pp. 247 ff.
47. *D.*49.15.12.1.

Chapter 2 Manumission and Citizenship

1. See, e.g., Appian, *Civil Wars*, 1.100, 104; Dio, *Roman History*, 55.26; J.1.42, 43; cf. Hopkins, *Conquerors and Slaves* (Cambridge: Cambridge University Press, 1978), pp. 115 ff. See also G. Alföldy, "Die Freilassung von Sklaven und die Struktur der Sklaverei in der römischen Kaiserzeit," *Rivista Storica dell'Antichità* 2 (1972): 97 ff; K. R. Bradley, *Slaves and Masters in the Roman Empire* (Brussels: Latomus, 1984), pp. 81 ff.
2. *Philippicae*, 8.32.
3. See, e.g., D. Daube, "Two Early Patterns of Manumission," *Journal of*

Roman Studies 36 (1946): 57 ff. See also Fabre, *Libertus*, pp. 10 ff, and the works he cites.

4. See, e.g., Watson, *XII Tables*, pp. 90 f; Buckland, *Slavery*, pp. 439 ff.
5. See, e.g., R. Reggi, "La *vindicatio in libertatem* e l'*adsertor libertatis*," in *Studi in memoria de G. Donatuti* (Milan: La Golliardica, n.d.), pp. 1005 ff.
6. For this view see, above all, Daube, "Two Early Patterns," at p. 63. See also Fabre, *Libertus*, pp. 16 ff.
7. See, e.g., Watson, *XII Tables*, pp. 86 ff; Buckland, *Slavery*, pp. 441 ff.
8. See, e.g., A. Watson, "Illogicality and Roman Law," *Israel Law Review* 7 (1972): 14 ff at pp. 16 f.
9. Cf. *D*.40.7.25; 40.7.29.
10. For the full argument see Watson, *XII Tables*, pp. 91 f.
11. See also *P.S.*4.14.1.
12. Aulus Gellius, *Noctes Atticae*, 5.19.13, 14; J.1.11.12. See the full treatment in Watson, *Persons*, pp. 90 ff: cf. Fabre, *Libertus*, pp. 37 ff.
13. *Topica* 2.10.
14. See also *Fr. Dos.* 4.
15. See also *P.S.*4.14.4; *Epit. Ulp.* 1.24.
16. For other evidence of large numbers of slaves see, e.g., P. A. Brunt, "Two Great Roman Landowners," *Latomus* 34 (1975): 619 ff.
17. See also *G*.1.44.
18. See also *Epit. Ulp.* 1.13; *Fr. Dos.* 13.
19. See *G*.1.21; *Epit. Ulp.* 1.14; *D*.40.4.27; J.1.26.1.
20. See especially *Gai Epit.* 1.1.2.
21. *C*.1.13.1.
22. *C*.1.13.1 = *C.Th*.4.7.1. Cf. J.1.5.1.
23. In general, Christianity left the legal position of slaves virtually unchanged; see, e.g., H. Langenfeld, *Christianisierungspolitik und Sklavengesetzgebung der römischen Kaiser von Konstantin bis Theodosius II* (Bonn: Habelt, 1977).
24. *G*.1.32, 32a.
25. *G*.1.32b.
26. *G*.1.32c.
27. *G*.1.33.
28. *G*.1.34.
29. Cf. *G*.1.17.
30. *C*.7.25.1 (A.D. 530–31).
31. *C*.7.3.1 (A.D. 528).
32. See also *C*.7.5.1 (A.D. 530).
33. *C*.7.5.1.
34. *C*.7.6.1 (A.D. 531).
35. *C*.7.3.1.1.

36. C.7.6.2.
37. C.7.3.1.5.
38. C.7.3.1.9.
39. C7.3.1.10.
40. C.7.3.1.11.
41. D.40.7.29.1.
42. D.40.7.2.pr.
43. D.40.7.3.

Chapter 3 Freedmen, Patrons, and the State

1. On the whole subject of freedmen see now, above all, Fabre, *Libertus*.
2. See also *Epit. Ulp.* 29.3.
3. See G.2.135–37.
4. See, e.g., G. Rotondi, *Leges Publicae Populi Romani* (Hildesheim: Olm, 1962), pp. 457 ff; P. Corbett, *Roman Law of Marriage* (Oxford: Clarendon Press, 1930), pp. 118 ff.
5. See also G.1.145; *P.S.*4.9.
6. See also the arguments of K. Atkinson, "The Purpose of the Manumission Laws of Augustus," *Irish Jurist* 1 (1966): 356 ff.
7. *Edictum*, p. 68.
8. The *formula* of the action against a freedman who disobeyed the edict is given in G.4.46. See also Fabre, *Libertus,* pp. 219 ff.
9. See D.37.15.2; 37.15.6; 37.15.7.
10. D.37.15.2.
11. It is often argued that the patron had the unfettered right to kill a freedman in the Republic and early Empire, but see, against that view, Watson, *Persons,* pp. 227 f; S. Treggiari, *Freedmen in the Roman Republic* (Oxford: Clarendon Press, 1969), pp. 72 ff.
12. *Coll.*4.4.2, 9.2.2, 9.3.3; D.48.2.8; C.4.20.12.
13. *Fr. Vat.* 272.
14. *Fr. Vat.* 308.
15. D.2.4.2.11.pr. The effect of this clause was disputed by the classical jurists Julian and Ulpian. Julian seems to have regarded such a marriage as subsisting despite the woman's attempt to dissolve it, whereas Ulpian seems to have taken the text to mean that the marriage was dissolved but the woman cannot remarry without consent; see Watson, "*Captivitas* and *Matrimonium*," *T.v.R.* 29 (1961): 243 ff at pp. 249 ff.
16. See also C.6.2.1.
17. D.37.15.5.
18. C.6.6.6.
19. *Coll.*9.3.3; *P.S.*5.15.3; D.22.5.4.

20. *Fr. Vat.* 309.
21. *D.*37.14.5.1.
22. *D.*37.14.18; see also 37.14.2; *D.*38.1.45. In the Republic it seems that such a prohibition was valid, but no action was given to a patron for breach; *D.*38.1.26; cf. Watson, *Persons,* pp. 230 f.
23. *D.*37.15.11.
24. *C.*6.3.13. Fabre believes that until the end of the second century B.C. the freedman was bound to reside with his patron: *Libertus,* pp. 132 ff.
25. *D.*38.1.2; cf. Lenel, *Edictum,* pp. 338 f. See also *D.*38.1.32; 38.1.36; 38.1.38.
26. See also *D.*38.1.34.
27. See also *C.*6.3.9.
28. See *D.*38.1.13.4; 38.1.30.1; 38.1.48.pr., 1.
29. See *D.*38.1.35.
30. *D.*38.1.13.3.
31. *D.*38.2.9.
32. *D.*37.14.6.pr.
33. *G.*3.56.
34. *G.*3.58.
35. *G.*3.63.
36. See, above all, on the whole paragraph, Treggiari, *Freedmen,* pp. 37 ff. But a *senatus consultum* A.D. 23 did declare that sons of freedmen could not be *equites.*
37. See, above all, A. M. Duff, *Freedmen in the Early Roman Empire* (Cambridge: Cambridge University Press, 1928), pp. 66 f.
38. Imperial freedmen could be very powerful, but they are a very special case and will not be discussed here.
39. See, above all, Watson, *Persons,* pp. 32 ff; Treggiari, *Freedmen,* pp. 81 ff; contra, Kaser, *RPR,* 1. p. 75.
40. Dio, *Roman History,* 54.16, 56.7.2; *D.*23.2.23; *h.t.*44; *Epit. Ulp.* 13.1.
41. *Naturalis Historia* (*Natural History*), 33.135.
42. *Naturalis Historia,* 33.134.
43. *Epistulae Morales* (*Moral Letters*), 27.5.
44. *Epistulae Morales,* 86.7.
45. Martial, *Epigrams,* 5.13. And one must not forget Trimalchio in Petronius, *Satyricon.*

Chapter 4 The Slave as Thing

1. Until the recognition of *peculium castrense* and *peculium quasi castrense* as giving some rights to the son.
2. See, in general, A. Biscardi, "La capacità processuale dello schiavo," *Labeo* 21 (1975): 143 ff.

3. That is, after the division into corporeal and incorporeal.
4. Greater precision is, I believe, not possible: see Watson, *XII Tables,* pp. 136 f.
5. Except for land, which could be mancipated at a distance: G.1.12.
6. See, now, A. Watson, *Law Making in the Later Roman Republic* (Oxford: Clarendon Press, 1974), pp. 32 f.
7. Reconstructed by Lenel, *Edictum,* p. 171.
8. See, e.g., F. de Zulueta, *The Roman Law of Sale* (Oxford: Clarendon Press, 1945), pp. 35 ff.
9. Aulus Gellius, *Noctes Atticae,* 4.2.1: see, on the edict, D. Daube, *Forms of Roman Legislation* (Oxford: Clarendon Press, 1956), pp. 91 ff; A. Watson, "The Imperatives of the Aedilician Edict," *T.v.R.* 39 (1971): 73 ff.
10. For noxal surrender, see chapter 5.
11. The text here is not in proper form: see, above all, B. Nicholes, "*Dicta promissave,*" in *Studies in the Roman Law of Sale dedicated to the Memory of De Zulueta,* ed. D. Daube (Oxford: Clarendon Press, 1959), pp. 91 ff.
12. Aulus Gellius, *Noctes Atticae,* 6.4.103.
13. *D.*21.1.28.
14. See also Aulus Gellius, *Noctes Atticae,* 4.2.9,10.
15. *D.*18.7.6; 18.7.9.
16. *D.*30.56.
17. *D.*30.45.1.
18. *J.*2.20.16.
19. Festus, *s.v. Talionis.*
20. *Coll.*2.5.5.
21. Aulus Gellius, *Noctes Atticae,* 20.1.12.
22. See, with references to earlier writers, A. Watson, "Personal Injuries in the XII Tables," *T.v.R.* 43 (1975): 213 ff.
23. Doubts have frequently been expressed: see, most recently, W. M. Gordon, "Dating the *lex Aquilia,*" *Acta Juridica,* 1976, pp. 315 ff.
24. See, above all, D. Daube "On the Third Chapter of the *lex Aquilia,*" *Law Quarterly Review* 52 (1936): 253 ff.
25. This last text seems rather confused, but see now R. Feenstra, "L'Actio legis Aquiliae utilis en cas d'homicide chez les glossateurs," in *Maior Viginti Quinque Annis,* ed. J. Spruit (Assen: Van Gorcum, 1979), pp. 45 ff.
26. See, above all, D. Daube, "Third Chapter," pp. 253 ff.
27. *D.*9.2.5 pr. (Ulpian, book 18 on the *Edict*); *Coll.*7.3.2, 3, 4.
28. This is basically the argument put forward by A. Watson, "*Contrectatio* as an Essential of *furtum,*" *Law Quarterly Review* 77 (1961): 526 ff at pp. 528 f. On this much controverted subject see, recently, G. Mac-

Cormack, "Definitions: *Furtum* and *Contrectatio*," *Acta Juridica*, 1977, pp. 129 ff; B. Nicholas, "Theophilus and *Contrectatio*," in *Studies in Justinian's Institutes in Memory of J.A.C. Thomas*, ed. P. G. Stein and A. Lewis (London: Sweet & Maxwell, 1983), pp. 118 ff at pp. 122 ff.

29. *Textbook of Roman Law*, 3d ed., rev. P. Stein (Cambridge: Cambridge University Press, 1963), p. 581.
30. *P.S.*2.31.19.
31. See, e.g., H. F. Jolowicz, *Digest XLVII.2, De Furtis* (Cambridge: Cambridge University Press, 1940), p. lix, and the texts he refers to.
32. See also *D.*47.10.15.43.
33. See also *D.*47.10.15.48.
34. *D.*11.3.5.3: See also Lenel, *Edictum*, p. 175.
35. See, on the whole topic, D. Daube, "Slave-Catching," *Juridical Review* 64 (1952): 12 ff. For runaway slaves in general see H. Bellen, *Studien zur Sklavenflucht im römischen Kaiserreich* (Wiesbaden: Steiner, 1971).
36. For the texts see Rotondi, *Leges publicae populi romani* (rpt. Hildesheim: Olm, 1966), p. 258 f.
37. *P.S.*1.6a.2.
38. See Daube, "Slave-Catching," p. 14.
39. Ibid., pp. 18 f.
40. By the time of Ulpian: *D.*48.15.2.1.
41. As Daube ("Slave-Catching," p. 25) points out, since the text talks of the "former owner," the sale to the slave catcher must have been valid, hence a device like that in *D.*48.15.2.2 must have been used.

Chapter 5 The Slave as Man: Noncommercial Relations

1. *G.*4.81.
2. *D.*47.10.17.4 ff; see also Lenel, *Edictum*, pp. 401 f.
3. *D.*47.10.17.4 ff; see also Lenel, *Edictum*, p. 402; Kaser, *RPR*, 1:632.
4. *D.*9.4.31; 47.6.
5. *D.*2.1.9.
6. See M. Bretone, *Servus communis* (Naples: Jovene, 1958), pp. 158 ff.
7. This translation takes, with Mommsen, the "*ut tibi soli serviat*" of the text as "*utri soli serviat*."
8. See also, e.g., *D.*10.2.16.6, 11.3.9.pr., and 47.2.15.36.
9. See, e.g., F. H. Lawson, *Negligence in the Civil Law* (Oxford: Clarendon Press, 1950), pp. 71 f.
10. See also *D.*9.2.27.9.
11. *G.*3.192–94.
12. See D. Daube, *Studies in Biblical Law* (Cambridge: Cambridge University Press, 1947), p. 269.

13. For a particularly strong example see G.3.198. Some texts do give a contrary view, e.g., *D.*47.2.43.pr., 1.
14. See, e.g., *D.*1.5.5.1.
15. *D.*18.1.5. For the development of the law of sale here see, above all, P. Stein, *Fault in the Formation of Contract* (Edinburgh: Oliver & Boyd, 1958), pp. 62 ff.
16. But see K. R. Bradley, *Slaves and Masters in the Roman Empire,* (Brussels: Latomus, 1984), pp. 47 ff.
17. *D.*23.2.45.6; *C.*5.16.27.
18. See also *C.*6.59.4, 6.55.6.
19. *D.*33.7.12.7.
20. See also *D.*33.5.21.
21. The same text appears in a rather different version in *C.Th.*2.25.1.
22. *D.*48.2.12.4.
23. *D.*25.4.1.10.
24. See also Bruns, *Fontes juris romani antiqui,* ed. L. Gradenwitz (Tübingen: Mohr, 1909), 1, 249; *C.*10.11.8.2.
25. See also *C.Th.*9.6.1; 9.6.3; 9.6.4.
26. *C.*9.8.3.
27. *D.*49.14.2.6.
28. *D.*5.1.53, 48.4.7.2, 48.10.7, 48.12.1.
29. *D.*48.10.7.
30. *P.S.*5.16.2; *D.*48.18.9.pr.; 48.18.20; *C.*3.32.10.
31. *D.*22.3.7.
32. See also *P.S.*5.16.1, 2; *D.*22.5.7.
33. See *C.*3.32.10.
34. *C.*9.41.13.
35. *D.*48.18.9.
36. To the best of my knowledge, this particular gulf is overlooked by modern Romanists. In modern French law there are restrictions on proving the existence of a contract which are quite distinct from the existence of the contract.

Chapter 6 The Slave as Man: Slaves' Contracts and the Peculium

1. See, in general, I. Buti, *Studi sulla capacità patrimoniale dei servi* (Naples: Jovene, 1976).
2. G.3.93.
3. G.3.114.
4. The argument here is based on the pattern of development of the praetor's Edict: see A. Watson, *Law Making in the Later Roman Republic* (Oxford: Clarendon Press, 1974), pp. 31 ff.
5. See also *D.*15.1.5.4.

6. *D*.15.1.52.pr.
7. See also *D*.15.1.7.4.
8. See, e.g., A. Watson, *Law of Obligations in the Later Roman Republic*, (Oxford: Clarendon Press, 1965), pp. 258 ff.
9. See, above all, on the action, Buckland, *Slavery*, pp. 166 ff.
10. See M. Finley, *Ancient Slavery and Modern Ideology* (London: Chatto & Windus, 1980), pp. 93 ff.
11. Buckland (*Slavery*, p. 189, n. 4) says that very little sufficed for a reservation to the master. But he has misunderstood *D*.33.8.19.pr.— not *D*.23.8.19.pr., as he prints—on which he relies.
12. See Buckland, *Slavery*, pp. 196 f.
13. See also *D*.41.2.24.

Chapter 7 The Master's Acquisitions through Slaves

1. See, e.g., D. Daube, "Fashions and Idiosyncracies in the Exposition of the Roman Law of Property," in *Theories of Property*, ed. A. Parel and T. Flanagan (Waterloo, 1979), pp. 35 ff at pp. 35 f.
2. See A. Watson, "Morality, Slavery, and the Jurists in the Later Roman Republic," *Tulane Law Review* 42 (1967–68): 288 ff at pp. 291 ff.
3. J. M. Kelly, as referred to by Daube, "Fashions," pp. 36 f.
4. See A. Watson, "Acquisition of Ownership by *traditio* to an *extraneus*," *Studia et Documenta Historiae et Iuris* 33 (1967): 189 ff.
5. *D*.41.3.41.
6. See *D*.47.2.14.17; 41.1.20.2; 13.7.11.6; and 6.2.7.10. Most modern scholars would put this development much later, but see A. Watson, "Acquisition of Possession *per extraneam personam*," *T.v.R.* 29 (1961): 22 ff, especially from p. 33.
7. See, in general, A. Watson, "Acquisition of Possession and Usucapion *per servos et filios*," *LQR* 78 (1962): 205 ff.
8. See A. Watson, "Acquisition of Possession and Usucapion," at pp. 214 ff.
9. See A. Watson, *Legal Transplants*, p. 33, and the sources cited in the notes.
10. See, e.g., W. W. Buckland, *Textbook of Roman Law*, 3d ed., rev. P. Stein (Cambridge: Cambridge University Press, 1963), p. 523; J.A.C. Thomas, *Textbook of Roman Law* (Amsterdam: North Holland, 1976), pp. 312 ff.
11. But the four consensual contracts, including sale, could be made without formality, hence in any way at all and thus in writing.
12. See also *D*.41.2.1.4; 41.2.13.pr.; 47.2.17.3; *P.S.*2.31.37.
13. *D*.41.2.13.pr.
14. *D*.41.2.1.14.

15. *D*.41.2.47.
16. *D*.41.2.47; 41.2.1.14; 41.2.3.17.
17. *D*.41.2.1.14.
18. See also *D*.37.11.2.9; *Epit. Ulp.* 22.13.
19. See *D*.29.2.51.2.
20. *Manuel élémentaire de droit romain,* 8th ed., ed. F. Senn (Paris: Rousseau, 1929), p. 873, n. 4.
21. *Slavery,* p. 140.

Chapter 8 Punishment of the Slave

1. Buckland, *Slavery,* p. 36.
2. *Infamia: Its Place in Roman Public and Private Law* (Oxford, 1894), pp. 63 ff. He cites no evidence. See also M. Kaser, "Der Inhalt der patria potestas," *Zeitschrift der Savigny-Stiftung* 58 (1938); 62 ff. at 73 ff; idem, *RPR,* 1:114, 284 (at p. 284 he says that censorian intervention is credible, even if there is no sure evidence for it); J.A.C. Thomas, *Textbook of Roman Law* (Amsterdam: North Holland, 1976), p. 393.
3. *Roman Antiquities,* 20.13.
4. Kaser, *RPR,* 1:75.
5. See T. Mommsen, *Römisches Strafrecht* (Leipzig, 1899), p. 24, n. 1.
6. See, e.g., T. Mommsen, *Das römische Staatsrecht,* 3d. ed. (Leipzig, 1887), 2:349.
7. For the facilities for torturing slaves, at the order of private master or public magistrate, to be provided by the holder of the public office of funeral undertaker, see lines 8–14 of the incription from Pozzuoli published by L. Bove in *Labeo* 13 (1967): 22 ff.
8. But Ulpian does: *D*.1.6.2.
9. On this rescript see also W. Williams, "Individuality in the Imperial Constitutions," *Journal of Roman Studies* 66 (1976): 67 ff at 76 f.
10. *D*.21.1.19.1.
11. For instance by Buckland (*Slavery,* p. 37), who accepts that Antoninus Pius's ruling on the subject restated existing law.
12. See also *D*.48.8.3.4; *P.S.*5.23.13.
13. See *D*.10.2.18.2.
14. It is widely held that from this time legal limits on the master's power to punish were more strictly imposed: see, e.g., Mommsen, *Strafrecht,* p. 617; Kaser, *RPR,* 2:126. C. Dupont suggests this was possibly due to the influence of Christianity: *Les constitutions de Constantin et le droit privé au début de IVe. Siècle: les personnes* (Lille: Klinksiek, 1937), pp. 31 ff. A very different view is that of G. Härtel, "Einige Bemerkungen zur rechtlichen Stellung der Sklaven und zur Beschränkung der Wilkür des Herrn gegenüber dem Sklaven bei der Bestrafung im 2/3

Jahrhundert U.Z. anhand der Digesten," *Klio* 59 (1977): 337 ff. He sees evidence that the economic crisis of the Empire led the ruling class to improve the position of slaves by law. He wrongly treats the *Digest* texts as if they are all the fruit of the second and third centuries.

15. But M. I. Finley does cite them as rulings protecting masters who had beaten their slave to death: *Ancient Slavery and Modern Ideology* (London, 1980), p. 122.
16. *Personnes*, p. 33.
17. See, e.g., H. F. Jolowicz and B. Nicholas, *Historical Introduction to the Study of Roman Law,* 3d ed. (Cambridge: Cambridge University Press, 1972), pp. 371 ff.
18. Though a failed prosecution after a complaint by a fellow citizen seems to be the background of the rescript of Diocletian of 285: *Coll.*3.4.1.
19. See also the rather modified version in *C.*1.4.1.
20. *C.*1.4.33.pr.
21. See D. Daube, "The Marriage of Justinian and Theodora: Legal and Theological Reflections," *Catholic University of America Law Review* 16 (1967): 380 ff.
22. See also *D.*48.3.2.1.
23. See, e.g., *D.*48.1.9; 48.1.11; 48.19.19; *C.*9.2.2.
24. For minor differences from the trials of free men, see also *C.*9.4.6.2,3.
25. *C.Th.*9.9.1; quoted on p. 15.
26. Pliny, *Epistulae* (*Letters*), 10.30 (Trajan). The rule does not appear in the *Digest. C.Th.*7.13.8 (380) may imply that slaves could not serve in crack regiments but might in others. The constitution is interesting as placing (in this regard) slaves on the same level as some free men, such as cooks and breadmakers: see V. Giuffrè, "Sui *servi* e la *militia* secondo il Codice Teodosiano," *Index* 8 (1979): 227 ff.
27. *C.*10.33.1,2.
28. *Novellae Theodosiani* 17.1. (439).
29. *C.*6.1.6.
30. *D.*43.24.11.7.
31. *C.Th.*9.10.4; *C.*9.12.8, 9.19.2.

Chapter 9 Senatus consultum Silanianum

1. *D.*29.5.5.2.
2. Tacitus, *Annales,* 14.42–45.